A COMPLETE GUIDE TO
RADIO CONTROL GLIDERS

A COMPLETE GUIDE TO
RADIO CONTROL
GLIDERS

George Stringwell

Nexus Special Interests

Nexus Special Interests Ltd.

Nexus House
Boundary Way
Hemel Hempstead
Hertfordshire HP2 7ST
England

First published 1997

ISBN 1-85486-144-1

Typeset by Kate Williams, London.
Printed and bound in Great Britain by Biddles Ltd., Guildford and King's Lynn

Contents

Introduction

Why build and fly a radio controlled sailplane or glider in preference to a power driven model?

There are almost as many answers to this question as there are R/C glider enthusiasts. However, if you ask a representative selection of 'glider guiders' to list the advantages of their particular obsession, certain common themes will emerge:

- Gliders are environmentally friendly – they are silent in operation, produce no noxious fumes and can be flown in areas of tranquil and beautiful countryside without detracting from the operator's or any other people's enjoyment of it.
- Many of the operational problems inherent with powered R/C models simply do not exist with gliders and sailplanes – for example, no vibration, no oil seepage, no engine problems etc. Gliders tend to remain in much better condition than the equivalent power model, and they last much longer. Indeed, given reasonable care and luck, an R/C glider can last almost indefinitely. The radio equipment itself also has a much easier life and is hence more likely to be free from failure.
- Other than the negligible cost of charging

the radio batteries (and the drive cells in electric soarers) there are no operating costs. This factor, coupled with the fact that the initial investment is lower due to no expensive IC engine being required, and the longer useful life span, gives a very high 'flying hour per pound' return. As an example, one of my thermal soaring models is now fifteen years old, is still using the same receiver and servos and has clocked up over 300 flying hours, despite being semi-retired for various periods. Apportioned over the original investment plus operating costs this is less than 50p per hour!

- Soaring can be as easy or as challenging as you wish. Flying a simple two-function model from a slope which is producing good lift is easy and relaxing. However, the same slope and lift can be used to perform complex aerobatics or fly detailed and beautiful scale models of full-size sailplanes or glider models of piston and jet prototypes. In other conditions, where the wind is light and the slope lift produced marginal, it can be a challenge just to keep a lightweight model airborne, and the sense of achievement when you can find lift and fly when everyone else is grounded is great. When flying a flat-field thermal or electric soarer, the challenge of extracting more duration from the same air than anyone else on the field, or, if alone, making this flight better than the last is an ever present one – or alternatively, if in a lazy mood, you can just enjoy adjusting the model to mostly fly itself and enjoy its smooth and graceful soaring flight with minimum interference from the pilot.

- A vast range of possible competitions exist – thermal duration and multi-task, various classes of electric soaring, scale flying, both from the flat (with aerotow or winch launching) or from the slope, multi model or single, against the clock, slope pylon racing, aerobatics, cross-country flying – the range is almost limitless.

I hope that the above has given at least an indication of why, after forty-eight years of aero-modelling, the last twenty of which have been largely devoted to R/C soaring, I still find new challenges and fascination in it, both in the workshop and on the field and slope. Over that period I have seen enormous developments in both the available range and performance of R/C sailplanes, and great technical advances in materials, radio equipment and aerodynamics. However, the basic challenge of using the air to extract the best performance from *your* model is unchanging and ever new – every flight is different, every flight adds something to your experience and skill.

If this book helps even a few more people get started in and enjoy the hobby/sport, and perhaps assists some enthusiasts in broadening their horizons and trying a different class of model or type of flying, then the effort of writing it will have been worthwhile.

Good lift and safe landings!

George Stringwell

CHAPTER 1

R/C soaring – a general background

This book will attempt to give at least some coverage to all aspects of R/C soaring; it is a big subject, and it will obviously not be possible to go into such depth of detail as, for example, my earlier book *R/C Thermal Soaring* which devoted over 400 pages to just one aspect. However, every attempt will be made to cover all the important points, and, where appropriate, further reading will be recommended.

Mention was made in the introduction of the many and varied classes of R/C glider. In order to better understand the scope of the sport, a brief outline of each class follows.

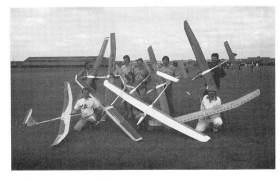

Collection of typical thermal soaring models.

General slope soaring

Any glider from the lightest to the heaviest can be flown on the slope in the appropriate conditions. For 'sport' many modellers have a general purpose type of glider which is at home in lift conditions varying from light to average; when the wind becomes very light it will either stop flying or change to a genuine thermal soaring type of model. Conversely, as the wind becomes stronger the heavier and faster multi-task and aerobatic types come into their own.

Slope aerobatic models

These are models equipped with full control in all axes – aileron, elevator and rudder, and often flaps and air brakes too. They range in size from very compact 'fun' models of no more than 3 feet span up to the very sophisticated and fast fibreglass moulded designs of 9 feet or more. Generally they feature a symmetrical or semi-symmetrical wing section so that inverted flight and 'outside' manoeuvres can be easily performed.

1

Simple basic rudder/elevator two metre model is the ideal type for a beginner.

Pylon race models and those designed to the F3F class rules

These are basically racing models; the pylon racers are flown over a course between two flags placed on the hillside, usually in groups of four on a knock-out basis. This can become very exciting indeed, but may also be rather damaging as the risk of mid-air collision is ever present. To reduce model mortality, the F3F contest was developed, this being basically a speed time trial flown one at a time over ten legs of a 100 metre

Successful thermal soaring competitor Bill Dulson with a large area aileron/flap model typical of the modern thermal soaring trend.

course. The performance of such models can be judged by the fact that times for the 1 kilometre course, including nine 180 degree turns, are regularly under 50 seconds.

Cross-country sailplanes

Designed to cover a cross-country course set out on the hills, flying through areas of sink or dead air and performing tasks en route, these models tend to be large and efficient. They are often very similar to the latest high performance full-size sailplanes in concept and appearance, usually feature technically advanced construction using composites and have a full range of controls including fully flapped wings to cope with varying lift conditions and wind speeds.

Scale models

These are miniature reproductions of full-size aircraft. They fall into two categories.

Models of full-size sailplanes
Often these are not so miniature, scales up to one-third full size are commonly seen with spans of up to 6 metres – 20 feet! Some outstandingly beautiful models have appeared, both of the very high performance modern glassfibre sailplanes and of the colourful and character laden wood and fabric types from the 1920s and 1930s. Naturally, many of these models can also be flown from flat fields using electric winch launching or aerotow by a power R/C aircraft.

Models of full-size aircraft which are not sailplanes
These are known by the acronym PSS which stands for Power Slope Scale. All types are seen from the monoplane fighters and bombers of WW2 up to the latest jet aircraft. Once again, some people build very large models indeed, but

Collection of glassfibre scale soarers await their turn on the slope or winch.

Flat field or thermal soaring

While almost any glider *can* be flown from a flat field, the performance of the heavier types designed principally to operate in the constant lift provided by a slope is likely to be disappointing. Consequently, while specialist thermal models, particularly the smaller ones, are often used for general flying on the slope in light wind conditions, or even for competition flights in slope cross-country events when lift conditions are especially light, it is rare to see slope models (other than scale sailplane types) being flown on the flat. Perhaps the exception here is the highly developed F3B or multi-task models, which make formidable slope pylon racers in just about any conditions, and are also capable of spectacular aerobatic performances in the right hands.

Perhaps more so than with slope models, the sailplanes used for everyday flying on the typical model club field tend to be very similar, if not exactly the same, to those which you would see at a contest. There are basically five distinct classes of specific thermal soaring model.

Hand launch or "mini" gliders

These comparatively tiny models, limited to a span of 60 inches and a maximum weight of 20 ounces, were originally intended for use in contests where the launch was purely by hand throw. Latterly, the rules were amended to allow use of a miniature hi-start or bungee line, which gave a launch similar to a good hand throw. However,

a typical PSS fly-in will see all shapes and sizes. Usually, as these aircraft are fairly heavily loaded, a decent breeze and good lift is required to allow them to perform to their full potential, although, by subtle 'stretching' of wings and slimming of fuselages, and the use of efficient lifting aerofoil sections, models can be produced which will perform in surprisingly light conditions. There are even two offshoots of this class – ESS, which stands for Experimental Slope Scale and encompasses models of project full-size aircraft that were never actually built (the latter WW2 period in Germany being a particularly rich source of these) and FSS – Feathers, Scales and Skin, in other words models of birds or flying reptiles.

*Beautiful scale **Olympia 2B** by Bob Goldman is an outstanding example of a designed from scratch model.*

3

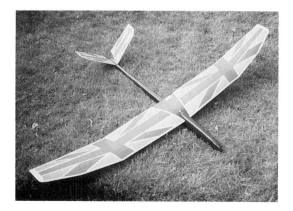

My little **Sundancer** *60 'V' tail* HLG *class – 16 ounces all-up weight, 60 inches wing span.*

the models are more often flown for pure fun, being cheap, easily transported and suitable for flying on any patch of open ground bigger than a single football pitch. They are normally simple rudder/elevator controlled models, built using traditional balsa wood modelling techniques and besides providing flying fun on the field, they are ideal 'holiday' models as they will perform brilliantly on any small slope.

Two metre thermal soarers

As the name suggests, these models are built to a span limit of two metres (79 inches). They are launched using an ordinary 150 metre towline or hi-start, and while sharing some of the advantages of size and economy with the hand-launch glider (HLG), the extra size does make them into very capable thermal soaring models. Unfortunately, there are few national contests for this class of model, but many clubs use them for their own internal events and they are, perhaps, the ideal model for the soaring beginner.

Standard class or 100S sailplanes

The genesis of this class dates back to the time when open class thermal soarers first began to grow in size, cost and complexity, the desire being to establish a restricted class which would

promote competition between models of reasonable cost. Over the years the rules have been subject to much amendment, including the removal of the original 800 square inch maximum wing area, so that now a 100S model need only have a maximum span of 100 inches and use rudder and elevator control only, plus optional air brakes (i.e. no ailerons or flaps are permitted). These rules produce a model which is large enough to be an extremely effective thermal soarer, capable of competing with almost anything in certain conditions, yet still reasonably cheap and simple to build and small and agile enough to fly from slopes in quite extreme conditions. Like the two metre model, this is a good type of sailplane for the thermal soaring novice.

Open and F3J thermal models

These are the aristocrats of the duration thermal soaring world, and are flown both in national open contests and those to the international F3J soaring rules. They are usually BIG – a 120 inch span open model is considered small, and 12 to 14 feet is normal. Generally they fall into two

Gordon Rae on the windswept Malvern hills with his **Skew Ball** *asymmetric tail slope pylon racer.*

types; the classic British light to middle weight open model will use rudder, elevator and air brake or spoiler controls and will usually be built in traditional style featuring spruce, balsa, ply and sometimes polystyrene foam materials, with perhaps a moulded fibreglass fuselage. The type of model that is becoming increasingly popular for the international F3J class, which demands faster towing and stronger models, is a more complicated design, often with full span adjustable flaps plus ailerons. Constructionally, more and more ready-moulded all-fibreglass models are becoming available, mostly originating from eastern Europe – at a price! Such models are wonderful performers in the hands of an experienced and competent pilot, but are best left well alone by the beginner or average club member.

Tough, glass-covered **Hatchetman 100** *standard class model by Alan Cooper.*

Multi-task or F3B gliders

Actually, the larger and more exotic moulded F3J models mentioned above owe their genesis to the multi-task type of model, and in general you would be hard put to distinguish the two types apart except for size. The F3B model tends to be rather smaller, typically between 2.75 and 3.5 metres span. The reason for this is that it is designed to compete in a class requiring three tasks to be flown – a 600 metre speed run, a distance task in which the greatest distance possible must be flown in four minutes and a duration task. These models are launched at very high speed by powerful electric winches and are extremely efficient, invariably featuring variable camber (flapped) wings with ailerons and sophisticated moulded composite construction. They also make superb fast slope soarers, competitive in racing and F3F events, and in cross-country events when the wind is strong and efficiency is at a premium. Superb but expensive flying machines which, again, are best left alone until a high level of pilot skill is attained.

As mentioned above, most scale sailplanes may be flown either from the slope or from a flat field; launching in the latter case will depend upon the size and weight of the model. Larger and heavier scale types will usually require either a power winch or an aerotow by a power driven model to produce satisfactory launches. However, models of older sailplanes with lighter wing loadings, even at all up weights of up to 10 pounds, can be satisfactorily launched by either an ordinary hand tow or, given a reasonable breeze, a strong bungee line. Once airborne, many scale models make very efficient thermal soarers and long, satisfying flights are possible.

Three other types of sailplane may be encountered flying from flat fields.

Vintage models

These are replicas of model designs which were first published before 1955. The originals were usually free-flight models, some of them very large, but the replicas use radio control. Naturally, these designs feature 'traditional' wooden structures, and the aerodynamic layout is such that they tend to fly very slowly. As a consequence they do not perform well in strong winds, but in light conditions they can be very satisfying indeed, and, in these circumstances, have often beaten modern machines in competition. However, the main motivation for building a vintage glider is not a competitive one, but rather a desire to see a piece of aeromodelling history in flight, and perhaps a nostalgic desire to recreate a model built in one's youth. There is actually a separate contest class run by BARCS (The British Association of Radio Control Soarers) for vintage models, and in this they compete directly with modern open models.

Tailless sailplanes

In some ways the tailless sailplane represents the purest form of model flight, and producing such a model which will deliver a performance equal to a conventional type is a challenge which some modellers find fascinating. Two types are generally seen – the straight wing 'plank', usually with rudder and elevator controls, which relies upon the use of a special reflexed section for its stability, and the classic 'vee' shaped swept wing which usually uses surfaces combining aileron and elevator functions (elevons) for control.

Self-launching sailplanes

By definition these may be any form of glider to which is applied some means of power unit to permit it to climb to altitude. This used to exclusively mean a small IC engine, either diesel or glow-plug type, but in modern terms is more likely to be an electric motor, probably incorporating a gearbox. Since, with the use of an IC engine, the model ceases to represent one of the most attractive aspects of glider flying, that of silent operation, it will not be considered further in this book. The use of electric power, however, is a quite different matter. Sailplanes are ideal vehicles for electric flight, and Chapter 16 is devoted to the subject. Electric soarers normally range from HLG size (60") up to around 100" span, although some very large scale models are seen equipped with power-

ful electric motors for flat field use.

From the above descriptions, it will be appreciated that the modeller who decides to make R/C glider flying his particular speciality in aeromodelling has a very wide choice of models indeed, and the contrast between, say, a 60 inch HLG and a 12 foot, all moulded, F3J type, or a slope F3F racer and an E400 class lightweight electric soarer is just about as great as you could wish, in both constructional and flying terms. It is also true to say that the flying experience offered by thrashing a fast aerobatic or pylon racing slope soarer around in strong slope lift and 30 knot winds is very different from that experienced when seeking out and working light thermal lift with a large 'floater' on a lazy summer afternoon – not better, or worse, just different!.

So large, in fact, is the choice of glider types that it is rare indeed to find a single modeller who flies them all at any particular time. However, since most thermal soaring types can be flown on the slopes in appropriate conditions, and lighter slope models will perform on the flat, many glider enthusiasts (unless living in, say, the heart of East Anglia where hills are rather scarce) dabble at least in both major divisions. Having flown all types extensively except the out-and-out F3B task model, I can thoroughly recommend trying several classes of model, at least until you are certain where your main interests lie.

The photographs in Chapter 16 are chosen to try to give an overall impression of as many of the different types of R/C sailplane as possible. The fact that a design appears here should not be taken to mean that it is necessarily the best in its class, simply that it is typical and hence gives a good idea of what you might expect in a model designed for a particular purpose.

CHAPTER 2

Weather and the model soaring pilot

As in the full-size world, the model sailplane pilot is much more dependent upon the weather conditions to provide satisfying flying than is the power pilot. This is the result of one simple fact – the unpowered model is always descending relative to the air around it. (Actually, it is not strictly accurate to refer to a glider as unpowered, it *is* powered – by gravity!)

It is obvious that to prolong the flight of the model, or provide it with the energy to perform aerobatics, we must find an area of air which is rising at a faster rate than the model's sinking speed. In this, the flat-field glider pilot finds himself in a somewhat different position from the slope soarer. In the latter case, no matter how miserable the weather, providing a wind of sufficient strength is blowing over a hill of the correct shape, rising air – lift – will be present. This applies even in a blizzard, and, in general, the only conditions that totally defeat the dedicated slope flier are those which involve either a total lack of wind (surprisingly rare in this country) or a lack of vision due to low cloud or hill fog. However, there is another limiting factor, and that concerns the physical endurance of the modeller. It is not particularly pleasant to stand on the edge of a hill facing a twenty knot wind in temperatures below about 50 degrees Fahrenheit. When the temperature gets down into the 30s there is a genuine risk of the incautious modeller suffering from exposure, so for those slope soarers keen on practising their hobby all year round, good protective clothing of the type worn by hill walkers is essential, with the emphasis on wind proofing. (The members of my club who indulge in winter slope soaring say that if you can recognise the person who is flying with you, they do not have enough clothes on!) There are compensations, however; the hills are less crowded in winter and, if properly prepared and protected, a couple of hours flying amid the winter splendour of the Peak District or Pennines can be extremely invigorating.

The thermal, or flat-field soaring pilot will find that there are a good number of days in the year when the weather is just not conducive to decent flying. Obviously, very strong winds pose problems, in that any lift that is present will be moving very rapidly downwind accompanied by considerable turbulence, but, strangely enough, extremely calm conditions, such as are associated with the presence of an anticyclone, can be equally difficult. The problem in this case is that there is no air movement, either horizontally to assist in obtaining a good launch, or vertically to prolong the flight. While thermal soaring is usually associated with sun and high temperatures, and it is true that the best days do normally occur in the summer months, lower temperatures and the absence of direct sunlight do not mean that there will not be usable lift available. Often, days with complete overcast will produce really excellent conditions for model soaring, especially if these are associated with a light wind.

Study of the general weather charts shown on the TV is likely to be of only limited use to the modeller trying to decide whether or not he will be able to go flying on the following day. These charts are extremely generalised; the wind speeds shown are subject, at the levels at which we operate, to considerable local variation in both strength and direction. In order to make the best of his soaring, the modeller needs to become something of an expert on his local conditions, and how these tend to vary from the general forecast for the area. What is required is a knowledge of the local *micro climate* in the flying area.

Some help can be obtained; local 'call-in' weather forecasts are a little more useful than the national ones, but not very much. Access to local airfield weather data, and in particular wind strength and direction, is rather more useful, but even this has to be interpreted in the light of local knowledge. Looking out of the window, unless you actually live on the edge of the slope or flying field, can be misleading. For example, I live on the western edge of the Derbyshire hills, and a pretty fair guess as to conditions in the hills can be made if a westerly wind is blowing. However, if the wind is anywhere in the east, it is very difficult to decide what one might actually encounter at the slope site. When I first moved into the area, I made many futile trips to the slopes, leaving home in flat calm equipped with a couple of lightweight thermal models, only to find a healthy twenty knot wind on the flyable slopes. After this had happened once or twice, I took to trying to second-guess the weather, and conse-

quently often ended up standing on the slope edge clutching a heavyweight aerobatic glider while facing the gentlest of zephyrs! The only real answer is to have one of everything in the car and decide upon arriving at the slope – although even this is sometimes not easy, as conditions in the carpark can be very different from those a couple of hundred feet higher up.

Assuming it is not actually raining (or snowing), wind strength is probably the single factor that looms largest in the R/C soarer's considera-

*A modeller prepares his **Eliminator** mini-glider under typical winter high-pressure sky with mares tail clouds.*

Competitors concentrating on their flying under a summer sky loaded with lift-marking cumulus clouds.

relying instead on the Beaufort wind speed system which relates wind strength to various observed effects, and it is given here together with general comments on the type of R/C gliding that might best suit the various conditions.

The specific effect of weather variations on lift patterns is discussed in more detail in the next two chapters, but generally speaking, thermal flying is pleasant in up to Force 3, possible up to Force 6 (and can even be enjoyable on a 'strong' day i.e. well defined lift – in such winds *if* a clean, fast 'task' type model, preferably with ailerons and flaps is available). Air movement and temperature variation are required to produce good lift, rather than extremes of temperature and sunlight. You can even find perfectly good and usable lift in the rain – if you are mad enough! Generally, freezing conditions, normally accompanied by calm or light winds, do not produce much in the way of thermal lift activity, being normally associated with anticyclonic conditions in winter. However, even the weak northern hemisphere winter sun acting on frozen ground can produce light lift around the middle of the day.

Slope flying, from a reasonable hill, is possible from the gentlest of air movement right up to near gale force conditions, summer or winter. Indeed, given the right model, the limiting factor is most likely to be, in winter, just what the modeller can stand. 'Good' hills, such as gently sloping sea cliffs produce lift in almost imperceptible drift conditions, but many hills will become turbulent and unusable over particular wind speeds. Once again, it is a matter of acquired local knowledge.

Reading the above in conjunction with the information on model types in Chapter 1, the conclusion will quickly be reached that, if the modeller is willing to build a few different types, he will be able to enjoy some soaring on the vast majority of days in a typical year. Calm evenings in the summer, or calm cold days in winter are ideal for the lighter thermal models. If launching is a problem then an electric soarer will provide the solution. Stronger winds mean any thermal

tion of weather conditions. Some people feel it is worthwhile to have a wind-speed meter of some description to aid in deciding which model might be right, or how much ballast to add. However, for slope soaring, this can backfire, in that the wind speed on the edge of the hill is likely to be very different from that fifty or a hundred feet above it. Even on a flat soaring field, there will be considerable 'ground effect' in stronger winds, and a reading of 10 miles per hour at head height may indicate double that figure at towline height. I have never bothered with a wind meter, model can be flown, or most slope types given a reasonable hill. Stronger still and the slope and multi-task 'hot ships' come into their own, along with all sorts of slope types including big scale glass sailplanes, PSS, aerobatic and racing types. The limit of weather in which one can fly is really decided purely by the individual, although during the novice and learning phases, it is wise to fly only in 'good' conditions. During my days of dedicated thermal soaring contest flying, I flew relatively light thermal models in some absolutely appalling conditions – but it was never something I particularly enjoyed! For the modeller intent upon 'sport' flying and enjoyment, it is better to try to 'go with the flow'of the weather, and, up to the point where physical discomfort decides that it is time to head for the fireside, try to match the model to the conditions rather than fighting to keep an unsuitable aeroplane flying.

There are a number of meteorology text books aimed at the full-size sailplane pilot that make interesting studies for the model soarer, although much of what they say is on rather too big a scale for us. Lately, with the rise in popularity of hang-gliders, para-gliding and microlight aircraft, there have been several works produced which concentrate more on the lower slice of the atmosphere which most interests us, so it is worth spending a little time browsing in one of the larger bookshops.

Above all, remember that, while our models might be miniatures, the air is full size. In other words, launching a twelve foot thermal soarer in a twenty knot wind is the equivalent of towing a full-size standard class sailplane in an eighty knot hurricane – not something that any glider pilot known to me would be in too much of a hurry to try!

The Beaufort Wind Speed Scale in relation to R/C soaring

Beaufort number	Wind speed (mph)	Description	Physical signs	R/C glider flying
0	<1	Calm	Smoke rises vertically	Electric, lightweight thermal soarer
1	1–3.5	Light air	Smoke drift, but wind not strong enough to extend flag	Electric, lightweight thermal soarer, HLG, very light model on slope
2	4–7	Light breeze	Wind strong enough to be felt on face, leaves in trees tremble	Any thermal soaring model, light to medium slope models
3	8–11	Gentle breeze	Light flags fully extended, leaves and twigs in constant motion	Medium and heavy thermal models, any slope model on GOOD slope, lighter models on poorer slopes
4	12–18	Moderate breeze	Small branches waving on trees, dust and paper lifted by wind	Medium and heavy thermal and task models, any slope soarer, PSS models
5	20–24	Fresh breeze	Small trees beginning to sway	F3B type thermal soarers, heavy scale, aerobatic, PSS and cross-country slope
6	25–30	Strong breeze	Larger branches in continual motion, wires hum	Heavy, clean slope models
7–12	32 plus	Near gale up to hurricane		Stay at home!

CHAPTER 3

Slope lift – how and why

It is a fact that many members of the public find the sight of a gaggle of slope soaring gliders effortlessly climbing and gyrating in front of a hill akin to magic. Even some experienced full-size pilots have a problem with the concept. I recall when a friend and I took a very experienced RAF pilot out for an evening's slope soaring at one of our more spectacular sites. As we stood, aerobatic models in hand, on the edge of the 500 foot drop facing a healthy fifteen knot breeze our guest said "You *surely* aren't going to throw them off *here*!" Needless to say we did, despatching the models in the approved fashion forty-five degrees down-ward, and his expression when they both shot up past eye level performing a series of rapid rolls was a picture!

So what is it that enables us to perform this apparent aeronautical sleight of hand? Try a simple experiment. Take an A4 sheet of card and a feather. Hold the card at an angle of forty-five degrees to the vertical, and then drop the feather above it. Move the card forward through the air towards the falling feather which will rise as the card approaches, eventually passing over the top of it. The card is your slope, you have created a wind onto it by moving it forward and hence

Terry Hoskins' version of Gordon Rae's **Finger One** *light wind model soaring on the Malvern Hills under cloudless skies.*

generated *slope lift*. It is as simple as that. Or, rather, it would be as simple as that if all slopes where flat planes angled at forty-five degrees with smooth surfaces and nothing in front of them onto which a steady breeze always blew at ninety degrees!

Thanks to the diversity of nature, we have a vast selection of different slopes, featuring every shape, angle, type of hinterland and surface imaginable. Most will only 'work' (the slope soarer's term for a slope which is producing usable lift) in a restricted range of wind directions, many will only produce lift, even with the ideal wind direction, at particular wind speeds.

The lift is created as shown in Figure 3.1. Essentially what is happening is that the air, as it approaches the hill, is forced to rise. The layers of air in contact with the ground will be moving somewhat slower than those above – a phenomenon known as 'ground effect', caused by the extra drag of the layers of air in contact with the ground – and hence, as the land starts to rise, turbulence will be generated in these lower layers. The amount of turbulence really depends upon how smooth the surface is – wind blowing across open water onto a shallow angled sea cliff shore-line will create very little turbulence. However, if the same wind were blowing onto the same shape hill, but over, say, a pine forest, then the turbulence might well be severe. As the hill rises, the successive layers of air are forced upwards, and it is this which creates a vertical component – the *lift* upon which we rely. Looking at the diagram, you will appreciate that as well as creating a vertical component, the wind speed will be higher at the top of the hill than it will be part-way down. Indeed, with some hills, it is quite possible to find a healthy breeze on the hill at the top has not only died away completely by two thirds of the way down, but might even appear as an eddy apparently blowing *away* from the hill near the bottom.

The above effect can be very important to slope soaring enthusiasts. It means that there is often a 'point of no return' on a hill – if the model is allowed to sink below a certain level there will never be enough ordinary slope lift for it to climb back up. As with most things in life, though, the news is not all bad! The lack of wind in the stagnant area at the bottom of the hill means that, if the sun is shining on the area, that mass of air warms up much more quickly than

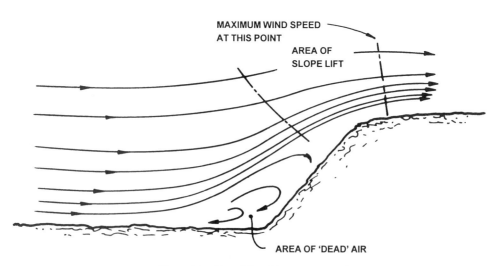

MAXIMUM WIND SPEED AT THIS POINT

AREA OF SLOPE LIFT

AREA OF 'DEAD' AIR

Figure 3.1 *Slope lift and how it is created.*

the surrounding areas and is hence a prime thermal generator – it creates what are known as 'wind shadow thermals', so the model sinking to the bottom due to lack of slope generated lift is sometimes rescued and wafted back to safety by a friendly parcel of warm air rising up the slope. However, we are getting rather ahead of ourselves, as this more properly belongs in the next chapter.

The strength of the lift generated, and its shape (i.e. how far above and in front of the hill it extends) will be influenced by a number of factors.

- The size of the slope – i.e. its height above the upwind terrain.
- The angle of the slope.
- The type of ground cover on the slope – trees, scrub, grass etc. will all produce different effects on otherwise similar slopes.
- Discontinuities in the face of the slope – typically gullies.
- The type of upwind terrain – is there another hill upwind, if so how far away? Or, is the run-in dead flat e.g. the sea.
- The wind strength.
- The angle of the wind to the slope.
- The shape of the slope viewed in plan view – is it straight (a ridge or cliff), or concave (a bowl) or convex (a rounded hill)?

- The general weather conditions – for example, on a day with large amounts of vertical air movement, that is a 'good' day from the point of view of thermal generation, the lift generated by the wind blowing on the hill will be reinforced or reduced (sometimes to the point of being cancelled out altogether) by thermals and downdraughts passing downwind.

The accompanying Figures 3.2 to 3.6 illustrate some typical slope shapes which will be encountered – these are, of course, 'idealised' versions, and every slope of a particular type will have its own peculiarities. The lift patterns indicated in the figures are merely indicative of what may be encountered, once again they will vary widely from slope to slope. It is this variability, where the lift produced by a slope may be totally different in character from what the shape and location of the site might lead one to expect which helps to make slope soaring interesting and challenging. Add to this the fact that further variations will occur, sometimes from minute to minute depending upon local weather conditions, and it is easy to appreciate that there is no substitute for local knowledge.

Slope soaring enthusiasts tend to be divided into two schools – those who seek reliable and constant lift so that their aerobatic, PSS or scale

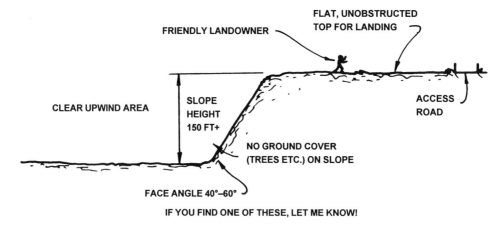

FRIENDLY LANDOWNER

FLAT, UNOBSTRUCTED
TOP FOR LANDING

CLEAR UPWIND AREA

SLOPE
HEIGHT
150 FT+

ACCESS
ROAD

NO GROUND COVER
(TREES ETC.) ON SLOPE

FACE ANGLE 40°–60°

IF YOU FIND ONE OF THESE, LET ME KNOW!

Figure 3.2 *Slope sites 1 – 'ideal' slope.*

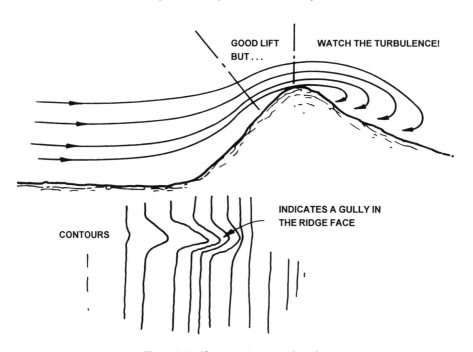

GOOD LIFT
BUT...

WATCH THE TURBULENCE!

INDICATES A GULLY IN
THE RIDGE FACE

CONTOURS

Figure 3.3 *Slope sites 2 – scarp/dip ridge.*

models may perform to maximum potential, and those who revel in the challenge of flying offbeat and sometimes unpromising slopes, and wringing maximum advantage out of less than perfect conditions.

Possibly the first thing to consider when surveying an unfamiliar slope site for the first time is not how good the lift may be – often the only way to establish this is to actually throw a reliable and well known model off the edge and try

14

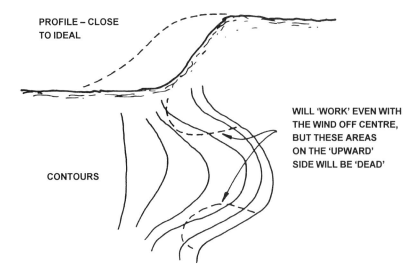

PROFILE – CLOSE
TO IDEAL

WILL 'WORK' EVEN WITH
THE WIND OFF CENTRE,
BUT THESE AREAS
ON THE 'UPWARD'
SIDE WILL BE 'DEAD'

CONTOURS

Figure 3.4   *Slope sites 3 – bowl.*

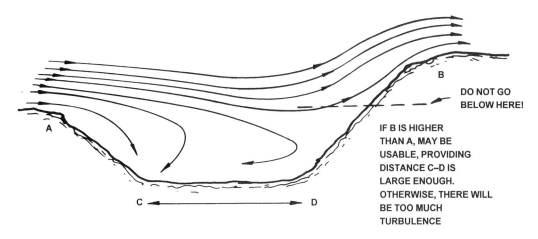

B

DO NOT GO
BELOW HERE!

A

IF B IS HIGHER
THAN A, MAY BE
USABLE, PROVIDING
DISTANCE C–D IS
LARGE ENOUGH.
OTHERWISE, THERE WILL
BE TOO MUCH
TURBULENCE

C   D

Figure 3.5   *Slope sites 4 – valley side.*

it (although the activities of soaring birds can sometimes give a clue; remember though that they have been doing it for millions of years, have an on-board computer and infinitely variable geometry wings, all of which factors help them in out-performing our poor wood and plastic imitations!) – but rather where will you land the model at the end of the flight. A glance at the diagrams will indicate that, if there is a lee slope to your particular hill, there will be downdraught and turbulence in this area, making landing there tricky. Similarly, landing on the top of a ridge, or the windward face of the slope requires a distinct technique which only comes with practice. Until

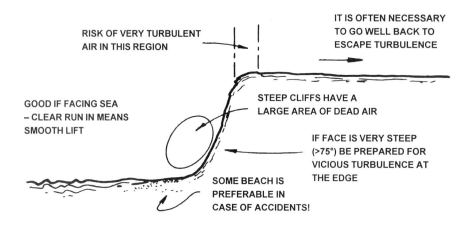

RISK OF VERY TURBULENT AIR IN THIS REGION

IT IS OFTEN NECESSARY TO GO WELL BACK TO ESCAPE TURBULENCE

GOOD IF FACING SEA – CLEAR RUN IN MEANS SMOOTH LIFT

STEEP CLIFFS HAVE A LARGE AREA OF DEAD AIR

IF FACE IS VERY STEEP (>75°) BE PREPARED FOR VICIOUS TURBULENCE AT THE EDGE

SOME BEACH IS PREFERABLE IN CASE OF ACCIDENTS!

Figure 3.6 *Slope sites 5 – cliff.*

A scale model is prepared for flight at Long Mynd, one of the best known model and full-size soaring venues.

skilled in all kinds of landings, the slope beginner would be well advised to stick to slopes with a nice, flat, area behind the ridge to provide an easy landing.

Once the soarer has mastered the art of ridge-side landing, then many more slopes are open to him; however, it is as well to remember that almost all land in this country is owned by some-one, and thus care has to be exercised in exploring that new slope. Also, local clubs often have harmonious relationships with landowners and they take a dim view of visiting or lone-hand soarers upsetting these due to lack of knowledge of local regulations. If in a strange area, the best place to ask is often the model shop in the nearest town, or, if you are going on holiday, the British Model Flying Association (see useful addresses in the Appendix) can provide a contact for the near-est club.

Many slope-soarers manage with just one model which they fly in all conditions. My per-sonal view is that much more enjoyment can be had with a few models, as the performance enve-lope can then be matched to the prevailing con-ditions. Fighting a twenty knot wind and strong lift with a 100 inch thermal soarer can be just as frustrating as scratching back and forth in near calm with an aerobatic slope model – reversing the roles will give two types of different but equally satisfying flying.

CHAPTER 4

Thermal lift – how and why

If the layman finds it difficult to understand how slope-generated lift works, he finds it even more puzzling when chancing upon a group of thermal soaring pilots flying from a flat field. The sight of a group of models spiralling upwards, sometimes at a considerable rate, in dead silence usually brings forth questions as to what they are powered by. As we said in Chapter 2, the answer, of course, is gravity!

For the modeller the detection and use of thermal lift is a more difficult and complicated question than that of finding a slope facing the wind which will more or less always give some degree of upgoing air. The rising parcels of air encountered over flat ground are invisible, with no apparent easy way to detect their presence, and they are always accompanied by equally invisible areas of sinking air which have a disastrous effect on the performance of the modeller's sailplane. However, as experience is gradually accumulated, it will become apparent that there *are* ways of predicting and detecting thermal lift, which is why the experienced thermal-soaring pilot finds some lift on a much greater percentage of his flights than does the newcomer, even if the latter is a competent R/C pilot and well versed in other forms of model flying. While detecting and

exploiting thermal lift is largely a matter of experience and hands-on practice, there are a number of basic 'rules' which will be of great help in the early stages, and these are discussed in detail in Chapter 13. The purpose of this chapter, however, is to give a general idea of what form thermal lift takes, and how it is influenced by factors local to a particular site and also the general weather conditions prevailing.

What is the elusive thermal lift which we are seeking? Well, as you would expect from the use of the word thermal, temperature is involved. Not absolute temperature; certainly, more lift is apparent on a warm summer's day, and the higher the angle of the sun, the greater its ability to heat up the ground and therefore the greater the likelihood of thermal upcurrents forming, but there is some usable lift for a model sailplane to be found in almost all conditions, as the important factor is *difference* in temperature. For a thermal up current to exist, we must have a situation where a volume of air is warmer – or, in winter, at least less cold – than the surrounding air. As we all learn in early science lessons, and the Montgolfiere brothers proved three hundred years ago, warm air rises. Since air cannot be heated directly by the sun, the heat must be acquired by the air being in contact with something else which can be warmed by the sun – the ground, or man-made features thereon. Hence we immediately have the beginnings of a way to predict the likely sources of thermals – ground areas which heat up more quickly than surrounding land.

So, a typical thermal generation scenario would be as illustrated by the series of drawings in Figure 4.1. Note that the volume of warm air in contact with the ground becomes larger until the whole bubble tears itself free and starts to rise. Once free of the ground the air within the thermal bubble will start to cool. However, as it is rising through air which is itself progressively cooler the further one gets from the ground, the temperature *differential* between the air in the bubble and the air surrounding it may very well *increase* as the bubble ascends. In other words, far short of slowing down as it goes higher, the rate of ascent will often increase – the lift will become 'stronger'. Obviously, if we can put our model glider, with a sinking speed of, say 1.5 feet/second, within such a rising bubble of air, providing the rate of vertical ascent of the air is greater than 1.5 feet per second, our model will, as long as it stays within the bubble, gain height. Notice that it is still descending relative to the air in which it is flying, as a glider, being gravity powered, *always* must.

Although, as mentioned above, rising air is generated to a greater or lesser extent in most weather conditions, there are obviously some which are much more favourable than others. Most people will be familiar with the fluffy fine weather cumulus clouds that march across the sky on hot summer days – these mark the top of developed thermals. While a warm day with the sky alive with cumuli is a good indication that there is likely to be good lift about, this kind of weather is not a prerequisite for the production of perfectly usable thermal lift for the modeller. Often the patches of lift which we can find and use never develop into the type of full-blown

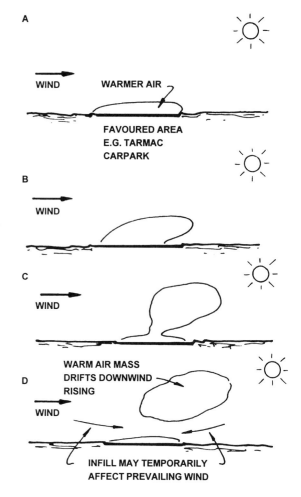

Figure 4.1 *Thermal generation.*

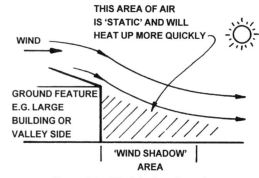

Figure 4.2 *Wind shadow thermal.*

thermals which the pilot of a full-size soaring sailplane will be seeking. The great enemy as far as the model flyer is concerned is *wind*. This is simply because of the need for the model to stay within range of, and return to, a fixed point on the ground – the launch point at which the radio transmitter is stationed. Naturally, any parcel of warm, rising air is going to drift downwind, so the higher the wind speed the faster it will drift and the shorter will be the time available for the ground-based model pilot to benefit from the rising air before his model must break away from it and return upwind to the launch point. Therefore, thermal soaring is inevitably easier in light wind conditions, indeed, as will be seen in Chapter 13, the wind itself can be an invaluable thermal indicator in these circumstances.

There are days when, due to the general high barometric pressure prevailing, the air is extremely stable in a vertical sense; these extreme anticyclonic conditions are usually accompanied (in this country at least) by calm weather – the type of cold, calm days that we often experience in late autumn and winter. These are not good days from the thermal soaring viewpoint, often there is no usable lift available, at least at the heights at which we operate, and flights are simply a matter of trimming the model for minimum sinking speed and gliding down from the top of the towline. Flying a line-launched glider can be rather boring in these circumstances, but such days should not be disregarded as the calm, stable air with lack of vertical disturbances offers the ideal opportunity to 'trim' a model to perfection, experimenting with subtle changes of balance point and flying surface incidence and observing their effects on the flight performance without the distortions caused by different types of air movement. As will be seen later, it should be possible in these conditions to adjust a duration type thermal soaring glider so finely that it will virtually fly itself with just minor inputs of rudder trim for directional changes from launch to landing.

Leaving aside the conditions mentioned in the previous paragraph, though, almost all days will produce some thermal lift at some time during the day. Even on one of the stable days mentioned above, if there has been any significant amount of sunshine, there will often be a sustained pattern of gentle lift in the hour before sunset, usually associated with certain ground features. The effect of the various ground features in general on thermal lift generation is dealt with in detail in Chapter 13.

Going back to our embryo developing thermal in the illustration, it will also be apparent that there is the reverse side of the coin. In the atmosphere, as in most things, there is no such thing as a free lunch, and if the body of rising air in which we are so interested is going to break free and rise (hopefully carrying our glider with it), other air will be drawn in to fill the space it has vacated. This infill of colder air will, inevitably, create areas where the air is moving downwards, which are bad news in terms of the modeller. On a strong thermal day, where large and violent areas of lift are encountered, there will be matching large and violent areas of downdraught. The art of avoiding these areas is just as much part of the model soaring pilot's necessary skills as is that of finding areas of upgoing air. As we will see later, the amount of time available to the pilot to recognise and react to 'bad' air is strictly limited, as the normal sink rate of the model can be multiplied by a factor of ten or more, coupled with associated handling problems. Fortunately, as the modeller becomes more experienced, he will become automatically attuned, without really realising it, to the likely lift/sink pattern in given circumstances, and will be able to assess the best area to fly through when leaving a thermal in order to avoid the sinking air which must be associated with it. Once again, there are hints and 'rules' to help while this unconscious awareness is acquired – see Chapter 13.

So, to summarise:

- The vast majority of days, winter or summer, are capable of generating some thermal lift. Except on rare anti-cyclonic calm days, the complaint "There is no lift today" can usually be taken to mean "There is no lift today *that I can find*!"
- It is easier to find and use lift in lighter wind conditions.
- Ground features will have predictable effects upon lift generation.
- The time of day is important – for given weather conditions, the lift pattern on any particular site will vary according to the time of day in a particular season.
- What goes up must come down – there must always be sink associated with lift – somewhere.

Realistically, on most flying fields, there will be an element of slope lift available in some areas. It takes only a surprisingly small feature, at right angles to the wind, to produce a band of rising air. This may be only a few feet wide and ten or fifteen feet deep, but it can be enough to keep a well flown light model airborne almost indefinitely. On my local field, a fifty yard long, twenty feet high, poplar hedge will, in a westerly wind, produce a standing lift feature which can be exploited by an HLG or two metre size model. Admittedly, a good level of skill is required to keep the model within the narrow lift band while making sure it is not blown back into the top of the trees during a turn, but several club members became so good at exploiting the lift that its use is banned in club contests! Such ground features can also play an important part in the formation of genuine thermal lift areas, as is outlined in Chapter 13.

Before leaving the general subject of flat-field lift, mention should be made of the phenomenon of wave lift. The best way of describing this would be that it is slope lift without the slope! Even this is not strictly true – there is a slope involved in the formation of wave, or lee wave, lift, but it may be many miles away. Many of the world's great mountain ranges, the Rockies being one example, will, given the right wind direction and strength, produce lee wave systems as illustrated in the diagram for hundreds of miles downwind. These are vast systems, with the effects stretching up many tens of thousands of feet into the atmosphere, and while they provide record-breaking opportunities for the full-size glider community, they are merely of interest to the modeller from an academic point of view. However, lee wave effect is generated by many smaller ranges of hills, including the Pennines, and these systems are on a smaller scale. At my own flying site, which is west of the Pennine/Derbyshire hills, once or twice a year a favourable set of circumstances and an easterly wind will combine to give distinct wave conditions. This can be

LENTICULAR CLOUDS IN LARGE SYSTEMS

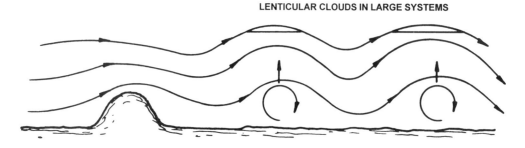

Figure 4.3 *Lee wave generation.*

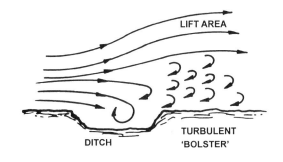

DITCH   TURBULENT 'BOLSTER'

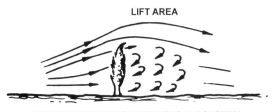

LINE OF THICK TREES PRODUCES A 'BOLSTER'
RATHER THAN TRUE SLOPE-LIFT EFFECT

Figure 4.4 *Small-scale ground feature lift effects.*

good or bad – in certain wind speeds the 'down' portion of the wave coincides with the flying field and when this happens the air is awful, it being a waste of time to even launch the model. Just occasionally, however, it is possible to get into the 'up' part of the wave from the top of a good tow launch (around 550 feet), although it is easier with a high climbing electric soarer, and then the lift is wonderful – smooth, powerful and seemingly endless, unless one is careless enough to descend too far and get below the bottom of the wave.

Of more interest, in general, will be the very localised wave effects which small hill features a mile or two upwind can produce. These often work right down to a couple of hundred feet and although the effects are small scale and require careful flying to exploit them, some interesting flights are possible on the flat field using this kind of lift.

CHAPTER 5

Getting started

If the introductory chapters have inspired a desire in some reader who has never previously built, owned or flown a radio controlled model sailplane to become involved in the hobby, apart from being pleased, I offer this chapter as the place to begin.

The first and most important advice that can be given to the absolute novice is; find someone in your area who knows what he is doing and get to know him! The simplest way to do this is to find out where the local club operates – often the nearest model shop can give you the details, if not try writing to the British Model Flying Association (see Appendix for address). They will be happy to give you details of the BMFA affiliated clubs in your area. Having found a group that flies the type of models which interest you (not all will, although most clubs have a spread of interest), visit a few of their flying sessions, make yourself known and express your interests. You will find most people are only too happy to talk about their hobby, and you will not be short of advice. Unfortunately, human nature being what it is, much of this might be conflicting! It is perhaps best to pick out one experienced modeller and, in the main, limit your queries to him. In this context, the man you are looking for is not

the one who talks the loudest or flies the lowest/fastest/longest, but the one who quietly gets on with his flying, has well built and finished models and takes them home undamaged at the end of the session! You will probably spot that he is also the one whose opinion is most frequently canvassed by other members.

If the foregoing paragraph implies that you cannot obtain a radio, buy or build a model and learn to fly entirely unaided without wrecking the model, well, it is possible – *just*! I have seen this done just once in thirty years. By far the safest and most sensible way is to seek and take advice about buying, building and, when the flying stage arrives, assistance in setting up the model and learning to safely fly and land it. Remember that even a small, lightweight radio controlled glider has the potential to cause extensive damage to property, or worse still, serious injury to people. (To illustrate this; a 28 ounce two metre thermal soarer belonging to me suffered radio failure at the top of the 150 metre towline causing it to descend vertically. This small, light model made a *fourteen inch* deep hole in the ground – which was not particularly soft – and the consequences of it striking a person were too awful to contemplate.) It is thus worth emphasising that you should *never* fly a radio control model without the appropriate third party insurance, and the easiest and most secure way of obtaining this is as a member of a BMFA affiliated club.

Having found a club, and hence a flying site, what will we need? First of all, a reliable radio outfit. Fortunately, we have now reached the stage where this is, almost, the least of our worries. Thirty-five years ago the radio side of the equation was still very much the province of the enthusiastic amateur electronic boffin. Many of the commercial sets available on the market were not totally reliable, and the better sets were mostly American and usually horrendously expensive. My first proportional radio cost the equivalent of two month's salary – now even the most expensive computer set would cost about one month's while the same amount would buy half a dozen basic, reliable and (for our purposes) perfectly adequate six-channel outfits.

Thanks to the tremendous developments which have taken place in electronics in the past twenty years, and the innovations of mass production seen in the Pacific Rim countries, any reputable commercial model control radio will offer solid, reliable performance at extremely reasonable cost.

For those coming entirely new to the subject, it might be as well to outline the layout and function of a modern, proportional, radio outfit. First of all, why 'proportional'? This simply means that the servo devices, which drive the model's control surfaces, move in direct response to the movements of the control sticks on the transmitter, in the same way that a full-size aircraft's control surfaces respond to the movements of the stick and rudder pedals. If you are feeling puzzled, because you could not envisage any other system, be assured that it was not always so easy! When I flew my first radio controlled model some forty years ago, proportional radio was, as far as the ordinary modeller was concerned, still the stuff of science fiction! Many were the weird

and wonderful switching systems used to produce viable model control sets – rubber and electric powered mechanical escapements, tuned reeds, tuned filters and many more. The one thing they had in common was that the movement of the control surface was *not* proportional to the movement of the control lever or button. Now, thankfully, things are a good deal easier; there is no other system to consider except proportional, and the requisite radio link can be bought from any model shop for a reasonable sum in the safe and certain knowledge that it will do the job.

Figure 5.1 shows the layout of a typical four- to six-channel digital proportional radio. As can be seen, the ground station is a handheld, lightweight transmitter, typically equipped with two dual axis stick units for controlling the four primary channels, and, if it is a six-channel unit, two auxiliary switch or lever units. The transmitter will also feature a meter which gives some indication of either signal output or (more usually) battery state. The unit will be powered by nickel cadmium rechargeable batteries (at the very bottom end of the market, some sets are available for dry battery operation, but the newcomer is **strongly recommended** to buy a set with rechargeable batteries and the appropriate charger). A collapsible car-type aerial is fitted, and the other features of the transmitter are likely to be largely related to the individual manufacturer's 'style'. Typically, switches will be provided to enable the control throw of the two main channels to be reduced to a pre-determined proportion of the full throw – 'rate' switches, and other switches (usually internally mounted) will be fitted to permit the direction of each of the channels to be reversed.

The airborne side of the outfit consists of a nicad battery (normally 4.8 volts and of 450–600 milliamp hour capacity i.e. pencell or AA size), a switch harness with socket for the battery, on/off slide switch and plug to fit the power socket of the receiver, a receiver (Rx) with a bank of sockets to

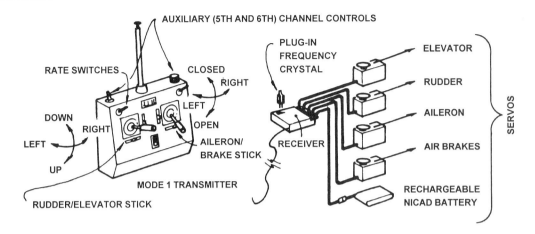

Figure 5.1 *Layout of a typical 4–6 channel digital proportional radio.*

take the power lead and servo plugs, a flex wire aerial and plug-in socket for the frequency crystal, and four or more servos, which are the electro mechanical devices that actually drive the model's control surfaces. A typical four channel airborne pack (i.e. nicad, Rx and four standard servos) will weigh around 280 grams (10 ounces), while a lightweight pack, with smaller Rx, more expensive mini- or micro-sized servos and small capacity battery pack (typically 225 milliamp hours) will weigh half this. For most soaring models, the standard size outfit is perfectly suitable, it is only when the modeller becomes involved with either lightweight or very small models, specialised electric soarers or the installation of small servos within the wing to drive flaps and ailerons that the lighter and more expensive equipment becomes necessary. Needless to say, all these developments should wait until the modeller has a sound grounding in basic soaring models.

A couple of recommendations here; unless the newcomer is very certain that he or she is going to be involved seriously in the hobby, probably in the competitive side, there is little point in buying the more expensive computer set at this stage. These sets have a microprocessor built into the transmitter, which is programmable to pro-vide various specialised functions – it can 'mix' the outputs of different control channels, for example aileron and elevator outputs can be mixed to give elevon control for a tailless model. It can alter the travel and endpoints of the various channels and adjust to give exponential outputs i.e. less around neutral becoming progressively greater with stick deflection. Many of these sets also have a memory facility so that the precise details of the set-up of two or more different models can be stored and recalled at will. Excellent as these facilities are, in the early stages they only cause confusion, and unless money really is no object (since the cheapest computer transmitter alone will cost perhaps twice as much as a *complete* four-channel outfit), the firm advice, for glider flying at least, is to settle for a sound, plain four- to six-channel outfit with two or more servos.

Conversely, while the early models which the newcomer is likely to fly will only require two channels of control – typically rudder and elevator – beginners are strongly advised *not* to buy one of the very cheap two-channel sets on the market. There are two reasons for this; first, complete control coverage for the type of advanced glider to which the modeller will hope-

25

fully progress requires three (rudder, elevator, ailerons) or four (the three listed plus air brakes or flaps) channels as a minimum, thus a two-channel set would be a poor investment, soon outgrown. Secondly, most two-channel sets are designed for use in R/C cars, and are hence on the 27 megacycle (MHz) frequency band. This is a 'mixed' band, theoretically available for both surface vehicle and aircraft control. However, no sensible model aircraft operator would use this band today, due to the great risks of interference, both legal (from surface vehicle users) and otherwise. Model fliers have an exclusively allocated frequency band at 35 MHz, and any set intended for aircraft use should be on this frequency band.

Two other considerations when purchasing the radio are those of **spot frequency** and **stick mode**. The 35 MHz band (which is the only one we will consider from now on) is split into 25 'spot' frequencies, separated by 10 kilocycles (KHz) and numbered 60 to 84 for identification purposes. In order for the radio to operate the correct and *matching* pair of crystals must be plugged into the transmitter and receiver crystal sockets. In theory this means that up to 25 models could be flown at any one time – but be assured that the sky would be very crowded indeed if this was the case. I have flown on several occasions with as many as fifteen other models, in thermal contest fly-offs and for sport from the slope, and in these circumstances the available area of sky seems very small and the proverbial 'eyes in the back of the head' would be more than useful! There are a number of important points regarding radio frequencies which the first time buyer of radio equipment should note. First, most soaring contests limit entries to using only the *even* numbered frequencies – 60, 62, 64 etc. This is a throwback to the days when power and glider radio contests often shared the same field (rare these days), when the power models would use the odd frequencies and the gliders the even ones. Many clubs, however, still expect glider fliers to use only even frequencies, so

before buying, do check with the club whose field or slope site you intend to fly at. Some clubs also maintain a register of members' 'preferred' frequencies, and reference to this before buying can avoid the newcomer buying a set of crystals for a frequency channel which is already heavily over-subscribed locally. Once established, the new modeller will probably wish to buy a second set of crystals so that, if there is already someone using his first choice he can still fly.

The second point on frequencies is one of great importance. All established clubs operate some form of frequency control. On lightly used slope sites this may simply be word of mouth, but is often a more formal arrangement involving a pegboard with a clip-on peg for each frequency. Confusingly, there are two distinct varieties of this system – one in which the pilot provides his own frequency numbered and named peg, and can only switch his set on when his peg is ON the board, and the other where a single set of numbered pegs is kept on the board, and the modeller may only switch on when he is in possession of the appropriate number peg i.e. it is OFF the board. Remember, if a set on the same numbered frequency as a model which is already flying is switched on, **control will be lost and the model will crash** with certainly damaging, costly, and possibly tragic consequences.

The importance of this business of frequency control is difficult to over-emphasise, so here are a few basic dos and don'ts which can save embarrassing and expensive accidents:

- DO always have a pennant on your transmitter showing the channel number of the crystal currently in it. DON'T forget to change the pennant when you change the crystal.
- DO take the time to become thoroughly familiar with the frequency control system in use at your flying site(s) BEFORE you operate your radio. Having done this follow the procedure religiously even if you are sure that there is no-one else present on 'your'

frequency – someone may have changed!

- NEVER switch on your radio in the carpark, or anywhere within range (say 1.5 miles) of a site where models may be flying.
- DO be sure to switch off your transmitter after flying; as an additional safeguard always collapse your transmitter aerial.
- DO be aware of what is going on around you; before switching on ASK.
- DO be careful when buying crystals that they are the correct type for your equipment – there are several different variations. For example, Sanwa crystals will not work in Futaba equipment.
- DON'T wander about the flying field with your transmitter aerial extended and set switched on – if a model on an adjacent frequency number passes close to your transmitter while it is relatively far away from its own, interference can result. In this case enlightened self-interest will indicate that you would be the nearest person to the out-of-control model!
- And finally, ASK and BE GUIDED BY the established and experienced members of the club.

The second decision to be made when buying the radio concerns stick configuration; since most sets can be changed from one configuration to the other it is not absolutely crucial, but it is better to buy the set in the configuration, or 'mode' that you will be using. Basically there are (for the right-handed pilot) two choices – throttle right or Mode 1, and throttle left or Mode 2. In Mode 1 the right-hand dual axis stick has the vertical sense non-self-centring, it stays where it is placed on a ratchet. The normal control allocation in Mode 1 is: right stick – horizontal axis for the primary direction control (either rudder or, if present, aileron), vertical axis for air brakes or flaps (throttle on a power or electric model); left stick – horizontal axis secondary directional control or unused (rudder on an aileron equipped model, unused on a rudder/elevator one), verti-

cal axis pitch control (elevator or all moving tail plane). In Mode 2 the horizontal axes remain the same, but the pitch control is on the right-hand stick (i.e. the same stick as the primary direction control, which is why Mode 2 is often called one stick) and the non-centring control of brakes or throttle on the left. A left-handed pilot would simply reverse the stick allocations in either case.

If you are a total beginner, you are by now probably confused as to which option to select. As a dedicated Mode 2 pilot for thirty plus years I have an interest to declare, but basically there are two factors which should influence your decision. If you are *very* right- or left-handed i.e. cannot write legibly with the other hand, or play the piano or easily do anything which requires that the two hands act independently, then you would probably be better with Mode 2. On the other hand, if you tend towards ambidexterity, then Mode 1 will suit you. However, more important is, perhaps, the mode which your selected mentor and tutor, and the rest of your new club use. While most clubs have a mixture of modes, and even some people who can happily fly either, it is very much a regional thing, and you could well find one club comprising predominantly Mode 1 fliers while 20 miles down the road their neighbours are just the opposite. Unless you have a strong preference one way or the other yourself, then it is best to ensure that there will be a number of instructors available to you who are happy and competent flying your chosen mode.

Having finally decided upon and purchased a radio outfit, the beginner now finds himself in need of a model in which to fly it. Specific advice will depend entirely upon the primary interest of the newcomer, whether he envisages that he will be spending most of his time flying from the slope or from the towline on the flat field. However, whether slope or thermal flying is contemplated, there are still basically three ways for the required model to be obtained Ready-To-Fly (RTF), Almost-Ready-To-Fly (ARTF) or kit/plan built.

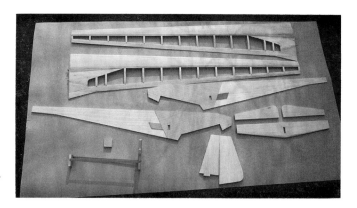

Component layout for simple Profile scale **Mucha** *standard slope soarer (my design).*

Until relatively recently the RTF route was only available via the purchase of a secondhand model from another modeller, or for relatively very expensive and usually fairly sophisticated models featuring such advanced techniques as moulded construction. However, with the change in the political situation in the Eastern bloc countries, and due to a greater focus on the RTF market in the Far East, some fairly conventional models which are entirely suitable for the beginner are available in RTF form at acceptable prices. Of course, what constitutes an acceptable price must be left up to the individual, but as a guide, it is currently possible to obtain a straightforward slope or small (two metre) thermal soarer completely built and finished in either wood or wood/foam/fibreglass for about the same price as one would pay for a four/six channel radio outfit to operate it. On these models the only work to be done by the purchaser is installation of the radio gear and setting up the control surface linkages and sometimes hinging control surfaces.

The other route to a ready-built model, that of obtaining one from a clubmate should not be disregarded, and some good bargains can be obtained this way. However, it is a little like the secondhand car market, and beware of the extravagant descriptions – "one careful lady owner, never raced or rallied" etc.! It is possible to pick up bargains, particularly in relatively sim-

ple models where the owner has moved on to more sophisticated types, but in general the advice is to only buy a model from someone you trust, and then only after careful inspection! One advantage of this route is that, if the previous owner used the same equipment – or at least the same size servos – as the buyer, then the control linkages and radio installation will most likely already be set up.

ARTF is a much abused term, and you will find that some kits which are described as ARTF require a great deal more work to get them to the flying stage than do others. For example, ARTF

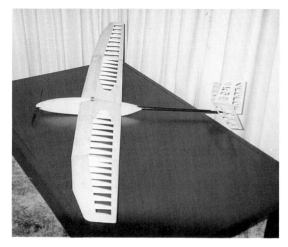

Neat and tidy structure of Australian Ian Haggard's version of my **Sundancer 74** *electric glider.*

Nice, clean lines on these basic thermal soaring models; the front one has built-up wings, while the smaller model has foam/veneer surfaces. Rudder/all-moving tailplane controls.

models very often feature foam/veneer wing panels. Depending upon the kit these may be supplied ready skinned but without leading and trailing edges fitted, with these components fitted but not joined, or ready joined for finishing. It is possible to buy an ARTF kit for a simple rudder/elevator slope soarer, for example, and have it in the air after two or three evenings' work. Another kit for a similar model, also styled ARTF, may require a fortnight of fairly intensive spare-time activity to get it to the same stage. Unfortunately, the difference in the degree of readiness is not always reflected in the price!

Beautifully built fibreglass fuselage 100S standard class model by Gordon Johnson.

When one then considers building a model from a more traditional kit – one which may or may not feature fibreglass mouldings and a mix of built-up wood or foam and veneer components, or from a published plan design, working from the drawing only and buying raw materials from the model shop, the available range of models becomes bewildering.

Once again, the best advice that can be given is to consult those who have already solved the problem. Most clubs and individual modellers will have experience of a range of designs, and will be able to help the newcomer in picking out the ones most likely to suit his needs, ability and pocket. After that it becomes very much a matter of personal preference, but do remember that, in a model intended to teach the basics of flying, good looks (the appreciation of which, in any case, vary from one individual to another) come a long way behind strength, ease and certainty of alignment and assembly and stable, forgiving, flying characteristics. There will be ample time to satisfy personal aesthetic tastes with later models which will not be subjected to the rough and tumble of learning to fly.

At this point, it might be as well to make it clear that there *are* some models on the market, RTF, ARTF and kit or plan designs, which are less than satisfactory in some aspect or other – sadly some of them in more than one aspect! For obvious reasons, names cannot be mentioned here, but once again, the local club members will

Tail end of a two metre **Gentle Lady** *shows how little wood need be used in a lightweight structure.*

know the worst offenders and be able to give a summary of the strengths and weaknesses of the rest. The only blessing is that, thanks to market forces, the less satisfactory offerings do not tend to be available for too long!

Whether the model is to be RTF, ARTF or built from scratch, the **type** of model which the absolute beginner first obtains needs to be carefully considered. If the newcomer is in the unfortunate position of having no easily accessible experienced instructor to guide him over the first flights, the only real chance of success is offered by choosing a model which has a good degree of automatic stability and will, if properly adjusted, correct itself if left alone. In this respect, whether the aim is slope flying or flying from the line, a model of between 60 and 80 inches span, with a polyhedral wing layout, reasonably slow (i.e. 10% thick or more) wing section and just rudder

and elevator controls is recommended. As a slope soarer this will need to be flown in light to moderate winds only, but it does offer the best chance of unassisted success. Typical of this breed of model are the *Orange Box*, available as a plan and the Goldberg *Gentle Lady*, a two metre span model available in kit form.

If regular and competent instruction is available, then a polyhedral wing rudder/elevator design is still recommended for starting in line-launched thermal soaring (indeed, many perfectly competitive thermal soaring models still do not use ailerons), but it can be of 80 to 100 inches span. A model like this will not only get the beginner past the learning to fly stage, but it will also be a useful tool for learning the elements of 'proper' thermal soaring – exploiting lift – and it will also be a useful model to fly from the slope on days when the wind and hence the lift are too light to permit use of the more heavily loaded specialist slope models. For the beginner who intends to specialise in slope soaring right from the start, and has an instructor 'on tap', then it might be worth considering a model around sixty inches span with ailerons – *not*, it should hastily be added, an out-and-out aerobatic type or pylon racer, but a model with a degree of stability such as the *Middle Phase* by Chris Foss, available as a kit (which can be built either as a rudder/elevator model or with ailerons).

The whys and wherefores of constructing (or, in the case of RTF and ARTF models, assembling) a model, installing the radio equipment, adjusting it for flight etc. will be covered in later chapters, but the newcomer will, hopefully, now have at least some idea of the type of radio equipment and model which he will need.

Bernard Doyle about to let go of his two metre model on the bungee line for another training flight.

CHAPTER 6

Considerations for flight

Assuming that you now have a model and radio equipment, it is now time to pause and consider a few basics about flight in general, and the flight of radio controlled model sailplanes in particular.

As already stated, the model glider will always be descending relative to the air around it, it will be using gravity as a source of power to produce forward motion through the air, and the flow of air over its wings will produce lift, so that instead of simply falling out of the sky as a piece of wood or rock does, it planes through the air covering distance. The wing of any aeroplane produces its lift by virtue of having a particular section, which, in causing the airflow to pass over it, generates a relatively lower pressure on the top surface compared to the bottom surface, and hence produces an upward force. A simple wing will generate lift, but it will be totally unstable and will descend in a twirling motion around its long (span) axis. To stabilise the wing, we add a further surface some distance behind it, the tailplane (more descriptively known in the USA as the stabiliser), or, in the case of the much less frequently seen canard airframe, in front of it, in the form of a foreplane. In order for the whole set-up to have positive (i.e. self righting) stability, it is normally necessary for there to be a difference between the angle at which the wing and tailplane are presented to the airflow – the angle of attack. Typically, the wing on a model will be set at a greater nose-up angle to the common datum line than the tailplane – the amount will vary, but on the type of models which beginners fly it will usually be between two and four degrees. Aerobatic models, on the other hand, where positive stability is a definite drawback, will tend to be set up with little or no incidence difference between wing and tailplane, to give a model which is neutrally stable. Add a nose in front of the wing for the purpose of getting the balance point sufficiently forward, and there is a conventional sailplane layout.

Much discussion will be heard among soaring pilots of the merits of this or that wing section, or aerofoil, but for the present, what we require is a section which is largely flat bottomed, has a maximum thickness of some 10 to 11 per cent of the wing chord (the smaller dimension of the wing) occurring around one third of the way back from the front (or leading edge). Some degree of upsweep on the bottom of the section approaching the front will usually be present. It is perhaps best to list some of the terminology applied to a model to help with this chapter.

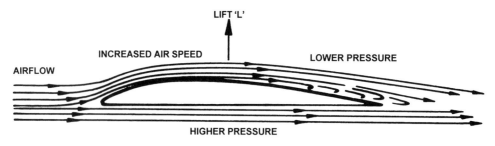

LIFT 'L'

INCREASED AIR SPEED   LOWER PRESSURE

AIRFLOW

HIGHER PRESSURE

LOWER PRESSURE ON TOP AND HIGHER PRESSURE
UNDERNEATH RESULT IN LIFT

Figure 6.1 *Creation of lift by an aerofoil section.*

Span   the tip-to-tip length of the wing.

Chord   the back to front width of the wing.

Area   the span of the wing multiplied by the mean chord, usually expressed in square inches or square feet in this country, and in square decimetres on the Continent.

Thickness   the depth of the wing section, usually expressed as a percentage of chord.

Leading edge   the front edge of a flying surface (and also the structural member found there).

Trailing edge   the back edge of a flying surface (and also the structural member found there).

Spar   the principal longitudinal (tip-to-tip) structural member of a built-up wing.

Rib   the fore and after members which give the wing section its shape.

Aspect ratio   the span divided by the mean chord of a surface.

Tail moment   the distance between the wing and tail of a model, should strictly speaking be measured between the quarter chord points of the wing and tailplane, but is often referred to simply as the wing trailing edge to tailplane leading edge measurement.

Nose moment   the length of fuselage nose protruding forward of the wing.

Dihedral   the angle at which the tips of the wing are raised above the centre. This may be via a simple join at the centre, or with multiple joins forming polyhedral.

Ailerons   the primary control surfaces in the roll axis, normally located outboard on the trailing edge of the wing.

Flaps   wing trailing edge sections whose movement affects the lift and drag characteristics of the wing and hence the whole model.

Air brakes or **spoilers**   devices which add drag and/or decrease lift produced by a model thus making steeper, slower descents and easier landings possible.

Rudder   the primary control in the yaw axis, usually located at the back of the vertical tail surface.

Elevator   the primary control in the pitch axis, usually located at the trailing edge of the tailplane. Deflecting this *down* causes the model to dive, up causes it to climb. Often, on model sailplanes, the whole tailplane is arranged to pivot – this is an *all moving* tail.

Wing loading   the total weight of the model divided by the total wing area. Normally expressed in this country in ounces per square foot, and on the Continent in grams per square decimetre. A lightweight thermal soaring model will have a loading of six to nine ounces per square foot, an aerobatic slope soarer or PSS model may go up to twenty to twenty-five ounces per square foot, and a pylon racer, loaded to fly in a strong wind, even higher.

The axes of control of an aeroplane – any normal fixed-wing aeroplane – are shown in the illustration. This refers to a model using ailerons for roll control – the model which the beginner will be flying, being a rudder elevator design will use the rudder as the primary, indeed the only, turning control. Hence it will have a relatively large dihedral angle on the wing, since it is only by having adequate dihedral that the rudder will give a satisfactory turning performance. In order to produce a properly co-ordinated turn – one in which the nose does not drop as the turn develops, and rise uncontrollably into a stall when the turn ceases, whether ailerons or rudder are used – co-ordinated use of the pitch control is also necessary, and this is probably the single hardest skill for the novice R/C pilot to learn

The layout of a model sailplane will vary with its purpose, meaning that all the above defined numeric parameters (span, chord, wing loading etc.) will typically be different for different classes of model. For example, an open class thermal soarer might have a span of around 140 inches, an aspect ratio of 16 to 18 to 1 and a wing loading starting at around 9 ounces per square foot and capable of being raised, with ballast to around fourteen or fifteen ounces per square foot. It may have rudder, elevator and air brake controls only, with a polyhedral wing to give adequate turning performance on rudder, or it may also have ailerons, and even full span flaps which double as ailerons, flaps and brakes. The tailplane area will typically be around 10 to 12 per cent of the wing area. An aerobatic slope model, by contrast, will probably span between 60 and 80 inches, have an aspect ratio of eight or nine, and an empty wing loading of about fifteen ounces per square foot, ballastable to twenty or more. It will have powerful, probably full span, ailerons plus elevator and a rudder, but may not have any air brakes. As can readily be appreciated, these are very different models and require very different flying techniques.

For the purposes of the newcomer, it is absolutely necessary that the first model, be it slope or thermal soarer, should have a degree of in-built stability – it should 'know' which way is up! This is because, in the early stages of learning to fly, the novice is going to be feeding in large and mostly unco-ordinated control movements and causing large disturbances to the model. If the model is neutrally stable to start with (for example, as a good slope aerobatic model will be – it will continue to go approximately in the direction it is pointed, whether this is up, down or sideways, until a command input from the transmitter instructs it to change heading) the newcomer is going to very rapidly get into trouble. He requires a model which, if left to its own devices, will right itself to approximate straight and level flight. These characteristics will most readily be found in a model with a largely flat-

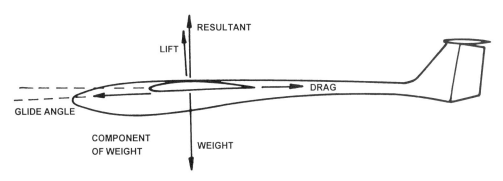

Figure 6.2 *Forces acting on a sailplane in flight.*

33

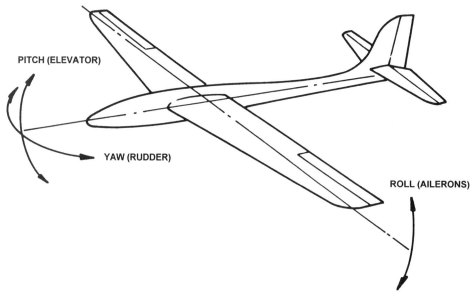

PITCH (ELEVATOR)

YAW (RUDDER)

ROLL (AILERONS)

Figure 6.3 *Axes of control.*

bottom wing section set up with a difference between the wing and tail angles of a few degrees, with the balance point (often referred to as the CG – centre of gravity) fairly well forward, probably about 30 per cent of the root wing chord back from the leading edge, and with a fair amount of dihedral to provide roll stability.

In setting up a model for initial flights, the main thing is to ensure that the wing and tail incidence angles and balance point are as shown on the plan, even if this means adding considerable ballast to the nose. The next thing to check is that the flying surfaces are straight and true when viewed from ahead, both in terms of their line-up with the fuselage and each other and within themselves in that no twist (warps) are present in them. Finally, the lateral balance of the model should be checked to make sure that one wing is not heavier than the other (add a small amount of weight to the lighter tip to correct this) and the control surfaces should be checked to ensure that they are central when the transmitter main stick

and trim controls are central. The amount of movement of the control surfaces should be monitored carefully; relatively speaking very little elevator movement is required to give quite violent pitch responses, whereas, on a typical rudder/elevator soarer, quite large rudder angles will be required to be effective. Almost all beginners' models which I have seen have been set up initially with too much elevator movement and often not enough rudder.

If the model is to a reputable design, and attention is paid to the above paragraph, it should (in calm to light wind conditions) hand glide from a smooth launch at a shallow downward angle without undue problems. If the model tends to stall i.e. it floats nose up and then suddenly drops, add a little extra ballast to the nose; if the angle of descent is a little steep, remove a small amount. It is better for the model to be a *little* nose-heavy for first flights rather than the reverse. Nothing more can profitably be learned from further hand glides, and the model should now be flown from

MEASURE A, B, C & D ON PLAN, THEN CHECK ON MODEL

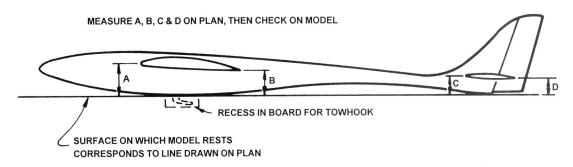

RECESS IN BOARD FOR TOWHOOK

SURFACE ON WHICH MODEL RESTS
CORRESPONDS TO LINE DRAWN ON PLAN

Figure 6.4 *Incidence checking.*

the slope or line by a competent pilot to check it out for any further necessary adjustments before the owner starts to learn to fly it.

Once the beginner has passed the stage of merely being content with the fact that his model will fly at all, and that he can fly it and land it, he will inevitably start to seek to extract the maximum performance from the model. While the type of beginner's model we are describing here is unlikely to be a world beater in the performance stakes, the difference between such a model well adjusted and flown, and one poorly adjusted and indifferently handled is striking. At this point we become interested in two particular aspects of a model's performance, which one becomes the most important will depend upon the type of flying we are doing. First there is the sinking speed. This is fairly easy to understand – if the model is launched from 500 feet and takes 4 mins 10 secs (250 seconds) to glide down to earth, the sinking speed would be 2 feet per second. Obviously, it is advantageous to have a low sinking speed, as this means that less lift, either thermal or slope, will be required to enable the model to climb. However, this is not the whole story, as very low sinking speeds in models are sometimes associated with wing sections which produce high lift at only one, relative slow air speed. If we vary the speed of such a model, as we will do when flying it under radio control, then the drag can rise very rapidly and the low sinking speed performance be totally destroyed.

The second performance factor which concerns us is glide angle. This is also easy to understand – if a model is hand launched from a height of six feet and glides for 72 feet before touching down, the glide angle is 72/6 or 12:1. In the full-size world, due to the type of task present day sailplanes now fly, glide angle is really all important, and the very latest high technology glassfibre sailplanes are capable of figures approaching or even bettering 50:1 – in other words, all things being equal, one could glide 50 *miles* from a five thousand foot launch. Model glide angles, even for the best and most sophisticated multi-task and slope cross-country models (classes where a good glide angle is particularly important) have yet to approach half of those achieved in the full-size glider world, due, mainly, to scale effect, but the best of these models are nevertheless very good indeed. The very flat glide also makes them quite difficult to fly, or at least to land, and good brakes and spoilers are necessary on such models. It will be appreciated that, without the use of some form of spoilers, a model with a 25:1 glide angle would need to be no more than 6 feet high when 150 feet from the landing spot – making it quite difficult to judge an accurate approach. Prerequisites for a good glide angle are a very clean airframe, a low-drag wing section and moderate to high wing loading. Since low sinking speed normally calls for lighter wing loading and slower flight with a wing section which will produce high lift, albeit accom-

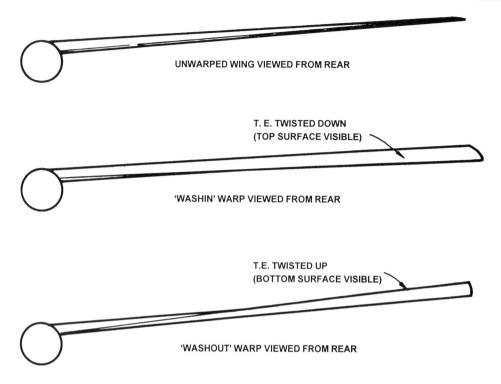

UNWARPED WING VIEWED FROM REAR

T. E. TWISTED DOWN
(TOP SURFACE VISIBLE)

'WASHIN' WARP VIEWED FROM REAR

T.E. TWISTED UP
(BOTTOM SURFACE VISIBLE)

'WASHOUT' WARP VIEWED FROM REAR

Figure 6.5   *Checking the incidence settings of a new model.*

panied by higher drag, then it can be seen that the two performance requirements are, to some extent, mutually antagonistic. Most models, much more so than their full-size counterparts where distance flying is now really the *only* criteria for contest success, tend to be compromise solutions between a decently low sinking speed and adequate glide angle.

In terms of what is most useful to the modeller, it depends upon the situation. If flying from the slope with very little wind and only light lift, you will be very happy if your model flies slowly and has a slow sinking speed. On the other hand, if flying in a strong wind which, due to not being quite on the slope, is producing less than adequate lift, a slow flying 'draggy' model will be a considerable embarrassment and you will be praying for glide angle – the shallower the better! Similarly, when thermal soaring, if you have followed some lift downwind, the low sinking speed of the model becomes fairly academic if it cannot be persuaded to fly fast enough and at a sufficiently shallow descent angle to get back to the field before it runs out of height.

CHAPTER 7

Some examples

In order to give some appreciation of the appearance of models typical of the various major classes of R/C gliders, this chapter contains layout drawings of typical examples. While other models of the same type will vary quite widely in overall dimensions and design detail from those illustrated, it will generally be found that the proportions, control layout and range of wing loading of successful models are fairly constant within each type. If, at a later stage of development, an own design is contemplated, these outlines will be a good place to start in order to ensure that the finished model has every chance of being a satisfactory performer.

First of all, layouts of two typical models which would be suitable for the beginner to soaring – one for slope use and one for towline flying, with use in light conditions from the slope as a second option. Figure 7.1 is an early design of mine, several of which have been built and used as initial slope soaring trainers by various newcomers to the hobby. Note that this is a very simple layout, with untapered wing held in place by rubber bands to give the necessary degree of flexibility in a hard landing (at first on the slope – and sometimes even later – most landings tend to be hard!). As previously mentioned, in models

such as this, elegance takes a back seat to functionality and ease of building and repair. *Snoopy* uses a very simple wing structure featuring hardwood spars for strength and a sheeted leading edge, top and bottom which produces a very rigid wing. The fuselage features sides laminated from ⅛" balsa with full length 1 mm ply doublers and the tail surfaces are all solid ¼" balsa for simplicity. An example using modern radio with two standard servos was recently built and weighed 26 ounces ready to fly with a wing loading of 10 ounces per square foot, making it a pleasant performer in light to moderate winds on any decent slope. At this weight it is capable of all the usual rudder/elevator aerobatics as the pilot's confidence increases.

The second model, in Figure 7.2, is the *Pastiche*, a design which was developed from the Goldberg *Gentle Lady* by a clubmate of mine, Len Whalley, and was much built by newcomers in the BATS club as a first thermal soarer. At two metres span, it is a compact model but one which will give an excellent account of itself against anything in the same size range in the hands of an expert thermal pilot. On the other hand, it is simple, strong and the flying characteristics are very forgiving, making it an ideal beginner's model.

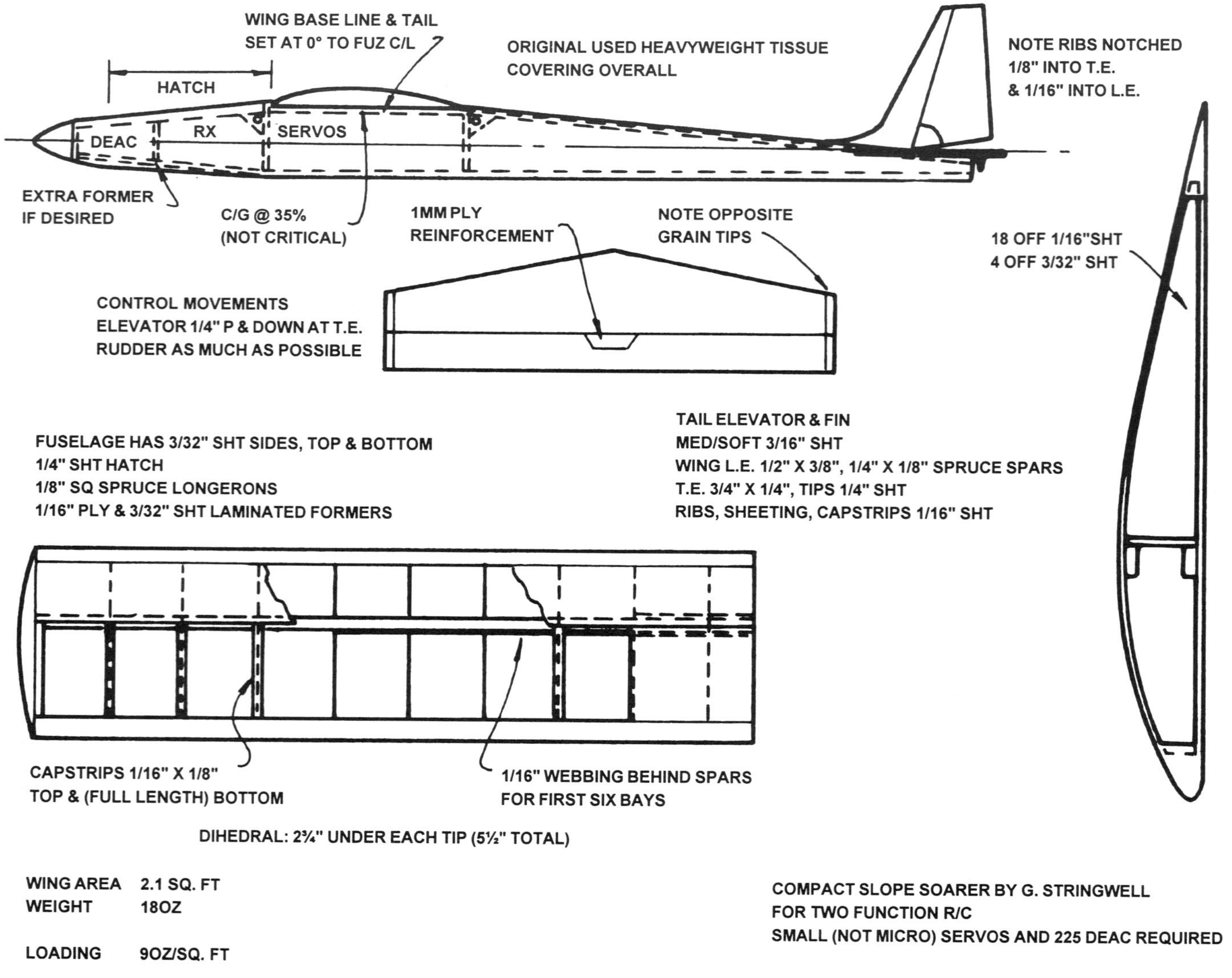

NOTE RIBS NOTCHED
1/8" INTO T.E.
& 1/16" INTO L.E.

18 OFF 1/16" SHT
4 OFF 3/32" SHT

ORIGINAL USED HEAVYWEIGHT TISSUE
COVERING OVERALL

NOTE OPPOSITE
GRAIN TIPS

TAIL ELEVATOR & FIN
MED/SOFT 3/16" SHT
WING L.E. 1/2" X 3/8", 1/4" X 1/8" SPRUCE SPARS
T.E. 3/4" X 1/4", TIPS 1/4" SHT
RIBS, SHEETING, CAPSTRIPS 1/16" SHT

1MM PLY
REINFORCEMENT

WING BASE LINE & TAIL
SET AT 0° TO FUZ C/L

C/G @ 35%
(NOT CRITICAL)

HATCH

RX

SERVOS

DEAC

EXTRA FORMER
IF DESIRED

CONTROL MOVEMENTS
ELEVATOR 1/4" P & DOWN AT T.E.
RUDDER AS MUCH AS POSSIBLE

FUSELAGE HAS 3/32" SHT SIDES, TOP & BOTTOM
1/4" SHT HATCH
1/8" SQ SPRUCE LONGERONS
1/16" PLY & 3/32" SHT LAMINATED FORMERS

1/16" WEBBING BEHIND SPARS
FOR FIRST SIX BAYS

CAPSTRIPS 1/16" X 1/8"
TOP & (FULL LENGTH) BOTTOM

DIHEDRAL: 2¾" UNDER EACH TIP (5½" TOTAL)

WING AREA   2.1 SQ. FT
WEIGHT   18OZ

LOADING   9OZ/SQ. FT

COMPACT SLOPE SOARER BY G. STRINGWELL
FOR TWO FUNCTION R/C
SMALL (NOT MICRO) SERVOS AND 225 DEAC REQUIRED

Figure 7.1 Snoopy II.

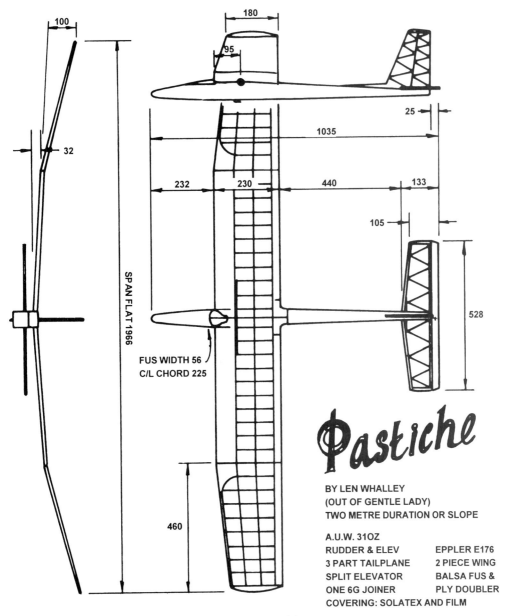

100

180

95

32

1035

25

232   230   440   133

105

SPAN FLAT 1966

528

FUS WIDTH 56
C/L CHORD 225

460

Pastiche

BY LEN WHALLEY
(OUT OF GENTLE LADY)
TWO METRE DURATION OR SLOPE

A.U.W. 31OZ
RUDDER & ELEV   EPPLER E176
3 PART TAILPLANE   2 PIECE WING
SPLIT ELEVATOR   BALSA FUS &
ONE 6G JOINER   PLY DOUBLER
COVERING: SOLATEX AND FILM

Figure 7.2   Pastiche.

The construction is entirely traditional, featuring a built-up wing with sheeted leading edge and spruce spars, balsa box fuselage with local ply reinforcement and tail surfaces built-up from strip balsa. With two-function radio the wing loading is around 7 ounces per square foot, making it ideal for the lighter conditions in which the newcomer will normally fly.

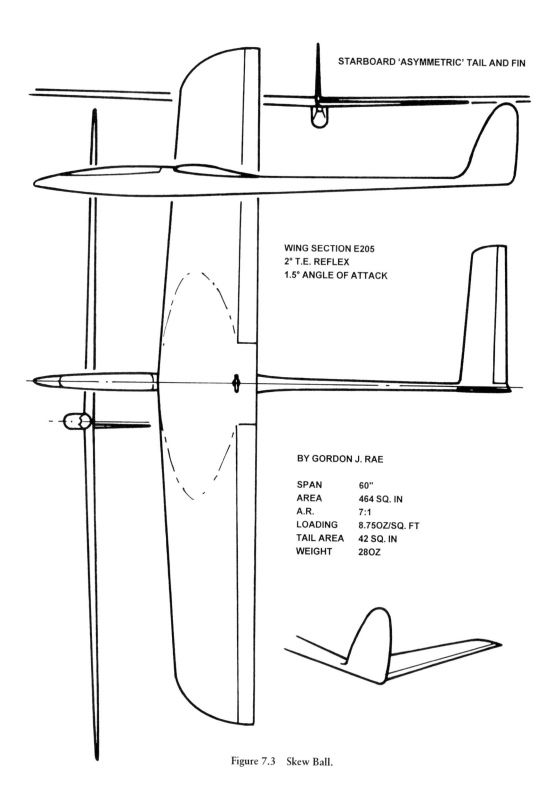

STARBOARD 'ASYMMETRIC' TAIL AND FIN

WING SECTION E205
2° T.E. REFLEX
1.5° ANGLE OF ATTACK

BY GORDON J. RAE

SPAN	60"
AREA	464 SQ. IN
A.R.	7:1
LOADING	8.75OZ/SQ. FT
TAIL AREA	42 SQ. IN
WEIGHT	28OZ

Figure 7.3   Skew Ball.

By way of contrast, Gordon Rae's 60 inch slope pylon race design in Figure 7.3 is a model of the type which the slope enthusiast might build as a third or fourth model, once he is proficient in basic flying. Although designed specifically for pylon racing in the limited span class, models such as these, by virtue of their compact dimensions, good speed range and crisp control responses, make ideal fast sport aerobatic slope gliders.

Dave Varah's *Big 'Un* (Figure 7.4) is a large, traditionally British, rudder/elevator thermal soarer. As you can see this is a *big* model, with a large amount of wing area. Designs such as this, albeit normally of slightly smaller dimensions (130–140 inches span), dominated the British thermal soaring scene for many years. In light to moderate conditions they are still capable of tremendous and contest winning performances and, being basically simple three-function mod-

els only require straightforward, inexpensive radio equipment. Once the thermal soaring pilot has cut his teeth on a smaller model and learned to really recognise and exploit lift, for sport flying in reasonable conditions a good big rudder/elevator open class model will provide spectacular flying.

Figure 7.5 illustrates the type of thermal soaring model increasingly seen in contests these days. Ben Clerx's *Mako* is much smaller than the previous design, and features a fully flapped wing (four micro servos in the wing alone), requiring computer radio to control it. It is really a hybrid machine, using design and structural technology developed for the international multi-task contest class (known as F3B) in an airframe bigger than the normal run of multi-task models to produce a fast, agile thermal soarer capable of handling the very strongest winds. In conditions up to about 10 knots of wind speed, such models

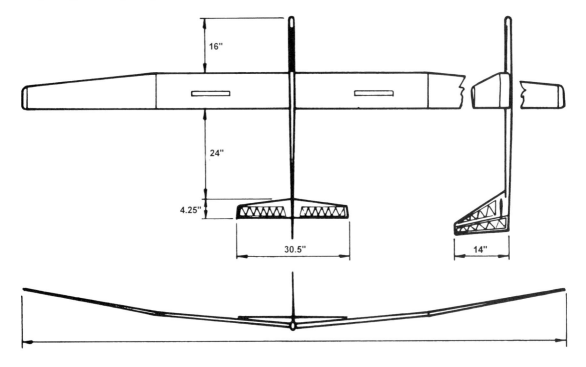

Figure 7.4   Big Un!

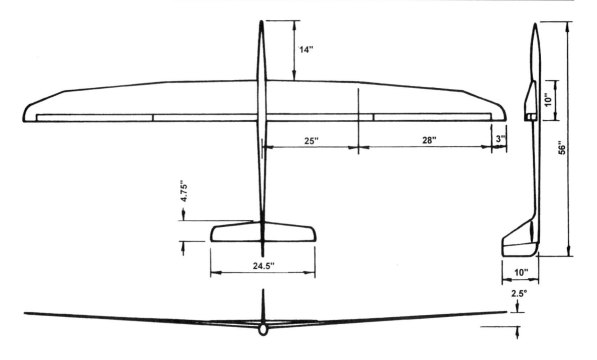

Figure 7.5   Mako.

have no advantage over the simple and usually larger rudder/elevator designs – indeed, their heavier loading makes tow launching more difficult and they are probably at a disadvantage in very light conditions. However, in higher wind, the superior glide angle and the availability of in-flight trim via the adjustable camber which the flaps confer enables them to very often get clean away in lift from their slower flying cousins. They have an additional plus in that their agility and glide angle make them very good slope soaring models, capable of a wide speed range and moderately aerobatic, while being able to stay airborne in much lighter lift than many pure slope models. Generally, the bigger rudder /elevator thermal soarers are only usable on the slope in very light conditions, as the typical turbulence found around slope sites in higher wind speeds can make these models, with their slower control responses, very tricky to handle.

The final illustration, Figure 7.6, is of a model for the hand-launch glider" or mini-glider class. This is another of my designs, this time a recent one, the 60 inch 'V' tail *Sundancer HL-V*. Originally, this class of model was developed for hand launching from the flat. In case the thought of simply throwing a model up to fifty or sixty feet and then finding a thermal and 'working' it away for a long flight sounds farfetched, please be assured it is perfectly possible for an experienced thermal pilot to do just this in reasonable conditions. The hand-launch rules were subsequently modified to allow the use of a mini bungee line which gave the less athletic modeller a chance to compete on equal terms with those having a strong throwing arm, as it gives a very similar launch, up to about 50 or 60 feet. The class is limited to a maximum span of 60 inches, and with an all-up weight of 17 ounces and a loading of 5.5 ounces per square foot, *Sundancer* is typical of

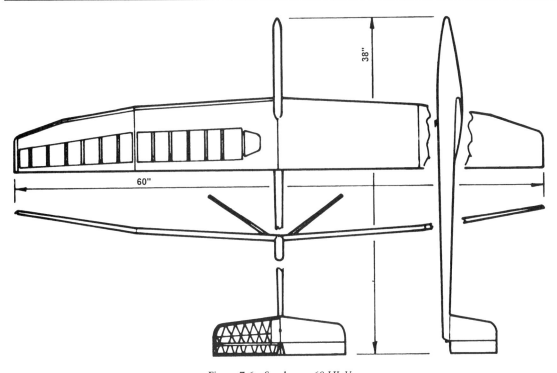

Figure 7.6   Sundancer *60 HL-V.*

the models flown. Requiring small servos and lightweight radio, these models are best left alone by the absolute beginner, but for the average pilot they can be a wonderful investment, not only for hand-launch flying but for launching from the full-size towline and slope soaring in the lightest and most difficult of conditions. A model such as this is an ideal holiday companion; it does not take up too much space in the car, and can be flown in those odd moments, either from the little bungee line or from small slopes (sand dunes and sea walls are two good examples) where the lift, although present, would be too light and tricky for a bigger or faster model.

The models described above and illustrated by the drawings are not presented as the best examples of their class, but rather as being typical, and to give an appreciation of the great diversity of shape and size which will be found in R/C sailplanes. Even in instances where models appear to be very similar, often the resemblance is only skin deep, with completely different wing sections being used which give very different handling and flight characteristics, while the range of structural options which can be applied to airframes of the same basic shape, from lightweight open-frame balsa structures through to fully moulded constructions in fibreglass, kevlar, carbon fibre and other sophisticated and exotic materials adds further variety.

CHAPTER 8

Construction techniques

As described in previous chapters, the extent to which the newcomer to R/C glider flying needs to become involved in the construction of his own models is, these days entirely up to him. It is perfectly possible for the R/C glider pilot, given adequate funding, to proceed from the basics of learning to fly right up to top level competition without the need to know any more about the design and construction of his models than how to install the radio equipment and set up the controls. In this sense it is now possible to treat the model glider in the same way as a golf club or tennis racquet – as simply a tool of the sport. Why is it then that most modellers still prefer to build their own models? Obviously, the question of cost must come into this, but there are many examples of R/C glider pilots who could well afford to buy the most expensive of ready-to-fly models, spending years of time and effort developing and building their own designs. The answer must only be that, like all other forms of aeromodelling, R/C gliding is a hobby which can be enjoyed on two distinct levels, and the satisfaction extracted from flying something which has been created with the modeller's own hands is still sufficiently great to attract most people.

With the exception of very few people, who are simply naturally talented craftsmen, the modeller needs to develop his building, and, perhaps, ultimately his designing skills over a number of years and via many different models. All the basic varieties of model aircraft construction can be found in R/C gliders, and this chapter will consider all the commonly occurring types and comment upon their suitability, their strengths and weaknesses.

The most important part of any model aeroplane, but particularly so in the case of a sailplane, is the wing, so this is a good place to start. Basic wing structures may be broadly divided into a number of types:

- All built up from balsa and hardwood.
- All built up from wood with load carrying spars from alloy or composite (e.g. carbon fibre).
- Hot wire cut foam cores married to wooden spar structures and skinned in wrapping paper.
- Hot wire cut foam cores skinned in balsa sheet or hardwood veneer.
- Hot wire cut foam cores with composite (veneer/glass fibre) skins pressed or vacuum bagged in place.

- Fully moulded hollow wings having composite stressed skins and produced in moulds.

Typical cross sections illustrating each of the above will be found in Figure 8.1.

Taking these methods in order, the first is also the most traditional and the basis of the wing structure will be recognised by anyone who built rubber powered flying models from kits during his youth. The wing consists of a number of longitudinal members – the leading edge (at the front), the trailing edge (at the rear) and one or more spars (in between), plus a number of evenly spaced crossways members, the ribs, which give the wing its aerodynamic cross section. The wing may be entirely open structure covered in tissue, fabric or plastic film, or it may be partially or fully sheeted with balsa sheet (usually 1/16" thick), depending upon the application.

The number and position of the spar members can vary widely, but the most commonly found, and one of the best structures, in R/C gliders is the 'I' beam spar with either partially or fully sheeted leading edge – see Figure 8.1. In this structure two spar booms, normally of spruce

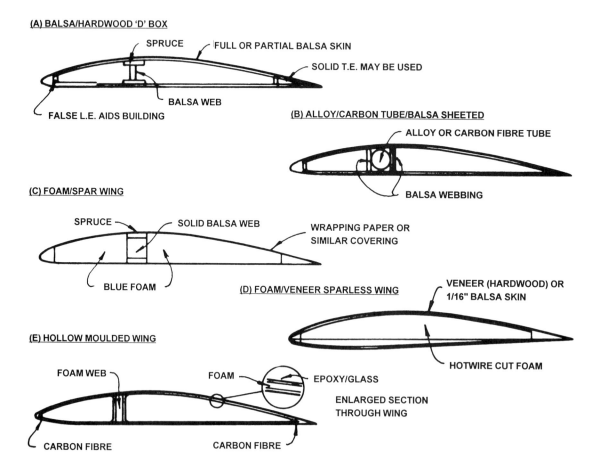

Figure 8.1 *Wing structures.*

unless the model is very small and light, are installed one above the other at approximately one-third wing chord and in between them is a spar web of balsa, locally reinforced at high stress points such as the centre section by ply. If the area between the spars and the leading edge is completely sheeted, top and bottom, then a structure known as a 'D' box is created, which has great bending strength. In the case of light-weight models either the bottom, or occasionally both bottom and top sheeting may be omitted to create a lighter, if less strong, wing. Returning to the normal D box wing, the ribs between the spar and trailing edge are capped with thin strips of balsa of the same thickness as the leading edge sheeting to form an even surface, the whole wing then being covered in a suitable material – mylar with tissue on top for lightweights, nylon or heat-shrink fabric or heat-shrink plastic film.

On larger models, or those where close adherence to the design wing section is a very important consideration, the whole of the wing may be sheeted with balsa, and in this case the dimensions of the spar booms will be reduced accordingly since the surface sheeting will be acting as a stressed skin, or distributed spar boom. In fact, on the wing tips of larger soarers, it will often be found that the spar booms are missing completely, with the structure comprising surface sheeting, spar webs and ribs only. The aim of this is to keep the wing tips light, which is a paramount consideration if the model is to have good handling characteristics in the roll axis.

The sequence of building a typical partially sheeted I beam sparred wing is covered by in Figure 8.2; as can be seen this is for a flat-bottomed wing which can conveniently be constructed on a flat building board. If the wing section with camber on the bottom surface, either positive (i.e. an under cambered section) or negative (a symmetrical or semi-symmetrical section) is used then some or all of the longitudinal members will need to be packed up the appropriate distance from the flat board to form a rudimentary jig. However, if the wing section has only slight upsweep on the front ten or fifteen per cent, with the rest substantially flat bottomed (as for example popular wing sections such as Eppler E205 and Selig-Donovan SD3021, both often used on thermal-soaring and general purpose slope-soaring models) then an alternative method can be used with the type of structure shown in Figure 8.2, in which the front lower leading edge sheeting is made of a thicker grade of sheet (normally $1/8''$) so that, while the wing is still built dead flat on the board, the upsweep can be carved in using templates for accuracy after the wing is removed from the board.

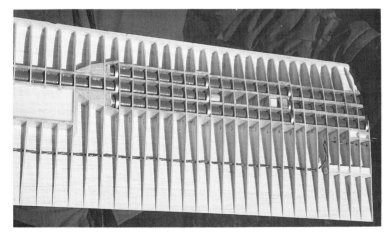

Immensely strong wing inner panel from Alan Cooper's **Hatchetman** *12 foot open thermal soarer before the top skin is fitted shows the alloy tube spar system.*

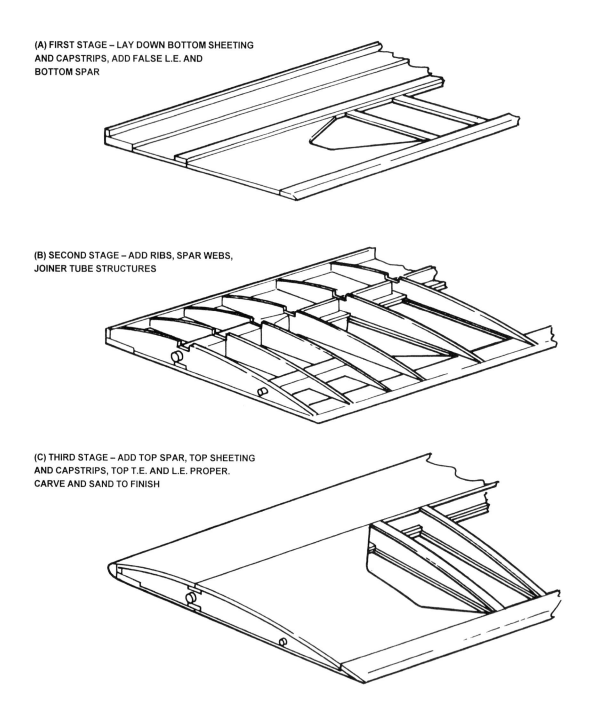

(A) FIRST STAGE – LAY DOWN BOTTOM SHEETING AND CAPSTRIPS, ADD FALSE L.E. AND BOTTOM SPAR

(B) SECOND STAGE – ADD RIBS, SPAR WEBS, JOINER TUBE STRUCTURES

(C) THIRD STAGE – ADD TOP SPAR, TOP SHEETING AND CAPSTRIPS, TOP T.E. AND L.E. PROPER. CARVE AND SAND TO FINISH

Figure 8.2 *Building sequence, spar/'D' box wing.*

Construction of a built-up wing using an alloy or carbon fibre tubular spar is very similar to the example shown, except of course that instead of the cut-outs in the surface of the ribs for the spar caps, a hole needs to be accurately made through each rib to accept the spar tube. Rather than having a single spar web to form an I beam, webs are fitted each side of the tubing spar. The tubular spar can serve two purposes in that it can carry ballast if it is desired to increase the model's wing loading for flying in windy conditions.

The most common form of wing encountered in the majority of RTF models and in many ARTF kits, especially those for slope soarers, is some form of foam cored structure. The foam used is of two types; blue or *Styrofoam*, as used extensively for insulation in the building trade, or the less workable and usually lighter polystyrene packaging foam – white foam. The cutting of wing cores from foam to any particular section is not a terribly tricky job, but it does require both the correct tools and a certain amount of practice. The cutting is carried out by a length of nichrome wire tensioned by a bow and heated by a direct current (normally 24 volts, sometimes 12 volts) passed through it from a transformer unit. Templates of the wing section at each end of the piece of wing being cut are fixed to each end of a suitable block of foam, taking care that they

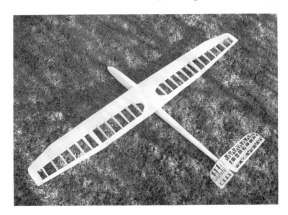

Lightweight structure of my **Sundancer 60** *HL-V HLG class mini-glider.*

are accurately aligned. Cutting itself is usually a two-man operation, unless one of the automatic cutting machines which are commercially available is used, and the aim is to pass the wire smoothly through the foam block around the templates, one surface at a time, creating a solid foam, aerofoil contoured core and two outer shaped pieces which are used to pack it (and in later stages of assembly).

It is debatable if the expense involved in obtaining the equipment and learning to cut cores is worthwhile for the individual modeller unless he intends to offer his services to others. Many clubs have one or more members adept at foam core cutting, and they keep all the others supplied. Additionally, there are a number of commercial operations who will supply cores cut to standard sections and lengths or to order from the modeller's own templates. If only cores are required, with no surface skinning, the cost is usually very reasonable.

Once in possession of the cores, these may be treated in a number of different ways to produce a finished wing, depending upon the type of model and application involved.

Medium-sized thermal-soaring models (up to 100 inches span) and general purpose slope soarers can use a wing which incorporates a pre-built full-depth spar unit, having top and bottom booms of flat spruce (commonly $1/8" \times 3/8"$ or $1/2"$) with solid balsa infill, the whole thing tapered to match the thickness of the wing section. A piece is then removed from the foam cores equivalent to the width of the finished spar unit, and the spar, front and rear core fairings, balsa leading and trailing edges are then assembled on a flat board on top of a sheet of polythene, and glued together either with thin epoxy resin or a suitable PVA glue. It is usual to use blue foam for this type of structure as it has a better surface, and once the glue is dry the wing panel can be gently sanded to remove any inconsistencies. White foam is usable, but it is much more difficult to work, tending to tear if sanded. Once complete, the wing is skinned with ordinary wrapping paper (either plain brown paper or patterned gift wrap can be used), using thinned PVA or even wallpaper paste as an adhesive. A coat of polythene varnish then produces a stiff and weatherproof wing for very reasonable weight and cost. If a two-part wing is required due to the size of the model, it is very easy to incorporate the main wing joiner into the spar before assembly. In view of the low cost of most of the materials, this type of wing is very suitable for beginners' models and trainers, being amply strong enough for the job providing the right spar structure is used, easy to repair and cheap to reproduce a spare part in case of a very severe crash.

One point should be made regarding the foam/spar wing described above, and that concerns the paper skinning. The skin is very important to the structure and it must be of a material which is going to provide sufficient stiffness to the wing. The spar, if properly designed and constructed, will take care of almost all the bending loads imposed on the wing, but it is the paper skin that must oppose the twisting loads. For this reason, although it is perfectly possible to cover this type of wing in heat-shrink plastic film instead of wrapping paper, this is definitely *not* to be recommended, as the film will add little in the way of torsional stiffness and the finished wing may well be subject to destructive flutter if flown a little faster than normal.

More sophisticated foam wings can be produced by skinning the foam cores with either thin veneer (usually obeche) or $1/16$" balsa sheet. As before, a balsa leading edge is normally used, and, sometimes, a trailing edge too. In the case of the wood skinned foam wing, it is not normal to build in any kind of full-length spar, as the aim is to produce a stressed skin structure with the wooden skin acting as a distributed spar. However, if the model is large (e.g., a two metre or more thermal soarer), it is normal to build the wing in two parts, and if a joining system is to be built in to this type of wing, it is essential that the bending stresses from the joiners are transferred evenly to the stressed skin, otherwise it is almost sure to break at the end of the joiner.

The normal way to achieve this is to build the joiner into a wooden and ply tapered sub-spar structure which is let into the core, either before skinning this with veneer or by cutting into the finished wing afterwards. The vital points in either case are to ensure that the spar/joiner structure does not end abruptly but tapers off and that it is well glued, not just to the foam core but to the surface veneer as well. It is normal to then reinforce the root area of the wing with a layer of thin glass cloth and epoxy resin, and this reinforcement should also be tapered off. For smaller wings – aerobatic slope soarers for example – it is usually sufficient to butt join the two wing panels with epoxy resin and reinforce the joint with glass cloth as described above. The function of the glass cloth in this case is to take the place of the

Sundancer 60 *E400 electro slot model under construction.*

50

wing joiner system on the large model and transfer the bending loads across the centre join from one panel's wing skins to the other.

The method of attaching the balsa or veneer to the foam core varies, the most popular (and the least strong) for home construction being to use an adhesive such as *Copydex*. Stronger, but infinitely more messy, is the use of a thin two part skinning epoxy resin such as *SP113*. If this is to be used, great care must be taken not to apply too much resin as this will result in extra weight rather than extra strength. The wooden skin must be evenly coated with resin, and then scraped or mopped to remove most of it and leave the thinnest possible overall coat. For heavy duty applications (slope pylon racing or multi-task soaring for example) a layer of thin (1 ounce per square metre) glass cloth can be laid up on the skin, in which case a further application of resin to 'wet up' the cloth will be required, again mopping away any excess. This, in effect, produces a composite skin, as such wings are usually finished with a further layer of the same glass cloth so that the skin becomes a glass/wood/glass sandwich, which is very strong and resilient.

Whatever method is used to apply the skin, the offcuts produced when cutting the cores (which are invariably included as protective packing with commercially produced items) come in very useful at this stage as simple presses. The method is to lay thin polythene over the bottom offcut, followed by the prepared bottom skin with adhesive, then the core (with any necessary additions such as joiner sub-spars, wing servo mounts etc. already fitted), then the top skin, followed by another sheet of thin polythene and the top offcut. As much weight as possible is then evenly added to this sandwich – the best way of doing this is to place a piece of chipboard over the foam pack and then add whatever weight is at hand (stacks of books are quite good) and the whole thing left until the adhesive is thoroughly dry (or cured in the case of resin).

The wing panels can then have leading edges added and be sanded to a finish.

One word of caution; both blue *Styrofoam* and ordinary white polystyrene foam are attacked and dissolved by cellulose compounds, therefore any cellulose-based adhesives (such as balsa cement and some contact adhesives) or finish (cellulose dopes) must be kept well away from the wing cores.

The remaining method of wing panel production, hollow wings with composite skins, laid-up and assembled in either glass or more usually metal moulds, is the province of either the talented and dedicated home experimenter who is seeking to develop and produce a sophisticated contest or scale model, or of the commercial concern whose aim is to produce high performance RTF models. The methods and materials used are almost the same as those employed in the production of full-size contest sailplanes, and the best models produced by these techniques are wonderful to both behold and fly, with breathtaking standards of finish. Mostly this type of structure is limited to the very large scale models (quarter and even third scale) of modern glass sailplanes produced on the Continent, or to the contest designs from the specialist manufacturers aimed at competition in the multi-task (F3B), slope speed (F3F) and international thermal soaring (F3J), and electric multi-task (F5B) classes. It should go without saying that, even if the finance is available, the newcomer should avoid models such as these until he is a competent pilot; they have breathtaking performance available in the right hands, but giving one to a newcomer to fly would be like expecting a learner driver to operate a Formula 1 car on his first lesson – with equivalent results!

The subject of joining multi-part wings was touched on above, but it is sufficiently important to require some amplification. Unless the modeller is either lucky enough to have a flying field in his back garden, or habitually travels around in a large van, any glider over about two metres span

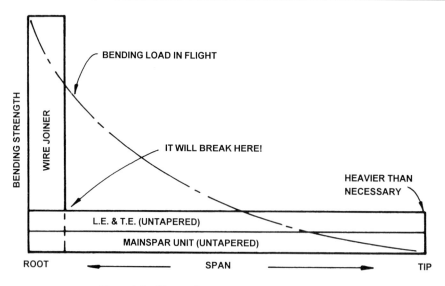

Figure 8.3 *Wing without tapered components.*

is going to require some method of joining a multi-part wing. The normal approach is to either to divide the wing at the centre and assemble the two panels 'plug-on' fashion to the fuselage, or, as an alternative, split the wing into three pieces with joints one third or so of the way out to each tip and a solidly assembled centre section which is bolted to the fuselage. The joiners used are the same in each case, the difference being only that the root type must take far greater bending stresses than the ones located farther out along the wing.

The aim of any joiner system should be to produce an assembled wing which is exactly the same in overall bending strength as if it had been built in one piece. This is not easy to achieve by any means. The problem is that the typical joiner – various sizes of spring steel wire, ranging from 10 swg for small models up to ¼ inch or even ⁵/₁₆ inch diameter for large thermal soarers, vertical spring steel blades or carbon fibre rods – is immensely stronger than the rest of the wing structure, and if inserted with no regard to tapering this strength out into the rest of the wing structure, it will produce a vast discontinuity at

the end of the joiner, which is just asking for the wing to break here. To illustrate this look at Figure 8.3. The curved line represents the distribution of bending stress along a wing semi-span – highest at the root, reducing to nothing at the tip. The straight lines represent the bending strength of the various longitudinal members – spars, wing sheeting, leading and trailing edge and, at the root, the joiners. It is easy to work out where the wing in this example will break – at or around point A. Now look at Figure 8.4 and note the difference which the addition of two tapered ply webbing pieces at the root has made. The wing will still break if it is totally over-stressed, but at least the end of the joiner is not acting as a stress raiser guaranteeing a break at that point.

When dealing with joiners outboard of the centre, as in the three-piece wing, much smaller section material can be used than at the root, since the bending stresses are much less at this point. However, the same principle of tapering out the strength into the rest of the wing structure applies.

Another factor which should constantly be borne in mind when building a wing is that of

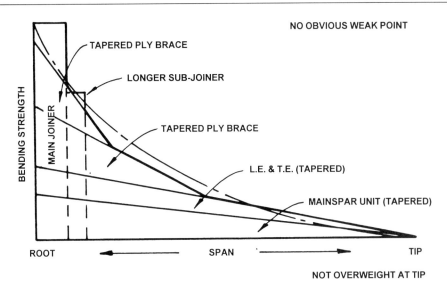

NO OBVIOUS WEAK POINT

TAPERED PLY BRACE

LONGER SUB-JOINER

TAPERED PLY BRACE

L.E. & T.E. (TAPERED)

MAINSPAR UNIT (TAPERED)

BENDING STRENGTH

MAIN JOINER

ROOT　　　　SPAN　　　　TIP

NOT OVERWEIGHT AT TIP

Figure 8.4　*Wing with tapered components.*

weight distribution along the span. Most model wings, if they are sufficiently strong at the centre section to cope with all reasonable loads, will be substantially over-engineered and hence heavier than necessary at the tips. Tapering the wing planform helps to some extent but it is also really necessary to taper the size and hence weight of all the main spanwise components too. On built-up and sheet covered thermal-soarer wings, for example, there are often no hardwood spar booms in the outer panels, as the sheeting itself is sufficiently strong to cope with the loads present this far out. Why is this so important? Try a simple experiment; hold a six foot long garden cane at its centre in one hand, horizontally. Now move the ends up and down by twisting the wrist. Add a small weight – an ounce or two – to each end of the can and repeat the twisting, noticing how much more force is needed to start the cane moving *and to stop it*. Translated into the terms of a model with heavy wing tips, this means that greater control inputs are going to be required to start and stop it rolling. In other words, handling in the roll axis will be much less crisp and precise

than the same model with a better lateral weight distribution. The penalties of heavy wing tips on a thermal soarer are imprecise and sloppy circling and slow response when trying to 'pick up a wing' on the landing approach, while in an aerobatic slope soarer they will mean that rolling manoeuvres lack precision.

Having considered the wing, it is logical to now examine the other flying surface – the tailplane. The problems encountered here are similar to the wing, but all on a much smaller scale! Due to the fact that the aspect ratio of the surface is much lower, bending and twisting loads are smaller, which is fortunate, as one of the most important characteristics of a tailplane is that it should be *light*. Due to the fact that it is between three and four times as far removed from the CG as the extreme nose of the model, every ten grams of extra weight in the tailplane will require three or four times that much extra nose ballast to compensate for it. While higher than necessary overall weight is therefore one consequence of overweight tail surfaces, it is not the whole story, as a model with a heavy tail end,

53

compensated by large amounts of extra nose weight, is going to have poor handling in the pitch plane – the situation is exactly the same as that described above for wing tips.

Whatever type of structure we select for the tailplane, therefore, a primary consideration must be to build it as light as possible consistent with doing the job.

Another consideration is the section of the tailplane. On present day R/C gliders (excepting vintage types converted to radio), it is unlikely that a tailplane with anything other than a symmetrical section (the same amount of camber on the top and bottom surfaces) will be found. Very often, even on quite large models, a flat plate section with rounded leading edge and tapered trailing edge is used. While this is convenient from a constructional viewpoint, it cannot be as effective as a proper section. However, on models where ultimate performance is not the aim – trainer and general purpose types – the convenience outweighs any efficiency considerations.

There are two types of tailplane to consider – the conventional elevator tailplane, where the pitch control surface is a narrow strip hinged onto the back of the tailplane, and the all-moving variety, where pitch control is obtained by pivoting the whole surface and then twisting it up and down. It is worth noting one important point about all-moving tailplanes here and that concerns the actual location of the pivot. This should be positioned so that between twenty and twenty-five per cent of the tailplane's area is in front of the pivot point. If the pivot point is moved forward from this location, the angular movement necessary to provide sufficient pitch response will increase until, if pivoted on the leading edge, very large angles will be required to generate the necessary pitch changes; large angles mean high drag and are hence not desirable. If the pivot is aft of this point, the opposite effect will be observed and the pitch response will become increasingly sensitive. There is, however, a further and more serious effect of the

pivot being too far aft, as the tail surface will become increasingly prone to flutter at higher than normal speeds, leading to failure of the mounting, control linkage or surface itself.

Generally speaking, the structures described are equally applicable to either all-moving or elevator tailplanes, although my favourite method described later is easier to apply to the all-moving variety. The options are:

- All-solid balsa sheet.
- Built-up open framework from balsa with hardwood reinforcement.
- Foam core covered with balsa or hardwood veneer.
- Foam cores skinned with glass cloth and resin skins pressed on.

Solid balsa sheet construction is only really suitable for use with flat-plate section tailplanes, as the weight penalty involved in using sheet thicker than ¼" is too great. This does not necessarily mean that the method is limited to small models only, as some thermal soarers of up to 12 feet span use flat-plate ¼" thick tails. Figure 8.5 shows the layout of a typical sheet balsa all-moving tailplane. The main body of the construction is from the lightest possible sheet (6 lb

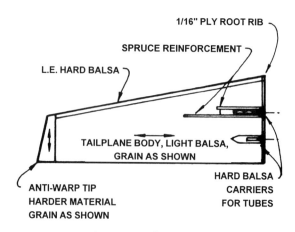

Figure 8.5 *All-sheet AMT.*

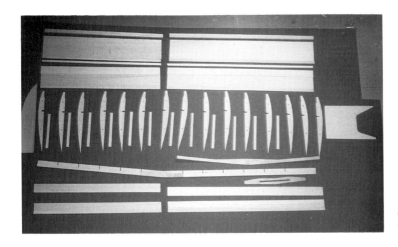

Component layout for one half of a **Clubman** *electric soarer wing.*

per cubic foot quality or less – see the table in the Appendix which gives weights for balsa sheets of various grades) while the opposing grain anti-warp tips and inserts and the leading edge are from a harder grade of sheet. With a thin sheet tailplane, some form of covering such as tissue and dope which will add more twisting strength than a plastic film type of finish, is desirable.

A built-up open framework tailplane, covered in either film, tissue or, for large models, fully sheeted, offers a way of producing a thicker section tailplane with a 'proper' symmetrical aerofoil for the same or less weight as a thin flat-plate all-sheet unit of the same area. As a straightforward and lighter alternative to the sheet structure described above, a built-up flat-plate tailplane of the elevator variety is shown in Figure 8.6. The diagonals are half the thickness of the leading and trailing edge members (i.e. $1/8"$ square for a $1/4"$ thick tailplane) and are glued

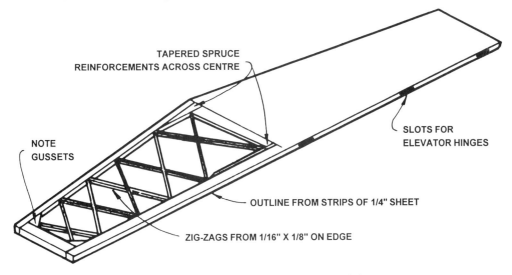

Figure 8.6 *Lightweight, flat, anti-warp tailplane.*

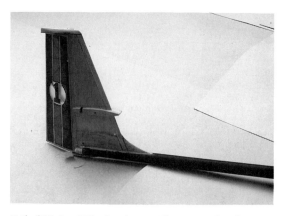

Tail of **Weekend Warrior** *shows mid mounting for all-moving tailplane and knuckle-hinged rudder (model also has ailerons).*

where they cross, producing a structure with good torsional stiffness and excellent strength/weight ratio.

To produce a full sectioned tailplane, a conventional structure, simply a small wing in fact, can be used. However, this is rather fiddly in the smaller sizes involved, and also requires a lot of jigging up from the building board to accommodate the symmetrical section. It also normally produces an over-engineered tailplane, stronger and heavier than necessary. I have used a method of producing light, full sectioned tailplanes for years now which gives outstanding strength/weight ratios and is particularly applicable to all-moving surfaces. The photographs show tailplanes of this type from two of my models; the larger one is for a 140 inch open class thermal soarer and the smaller one is for the *Sundancer 74* 400 class electric soarer. The V tail shows that the method can also be used, with some adaptation, for an elevator tailplane, this particular one is the 60 inch mini-glider *Sundancer*.

The basic construction technique is illustrated in Figure 8.7. The basic thickness chosen for the leading and trailing edge members will depend upon the size of tailplane to be produced, as an indication the smaller of the two in the photo-

graphs starts out at $^3/_{16}$" thick while the larger one is $^1/_4$" thick. The leading edge and tips can simply be cut from balsa of the appropriate thickness, but a much neater and stronger result is obtained if it is laminated from strips of $^1/_{32}$" balsa (6 strips $^3/_{16}$" wide or 8 strips $^1/_4$" wide), in which case the tips are integral. The laminations are soaked in water, and then pinned around a thick card former until dry. They can then be coated with aliphatic resin glue (PVA is not recommended for this application as it does not sand well) and re-pinned in place, truing it up by sanding once the glue is dry (leave the leading edge as a square section until assembly of the tailplane is complete). The straight trailing edge is cut from sheet of the appropriate thickness (8–10 lb cu ft grade).

The assembly sequence is as follows:

1. Pin down the leading and trailing edge, gluing where they meet.
2. Glue and pin down the bottom centre section sheet.
3. Glue and pin down the bottom diagonals ($^1/_{16}$" strip, either $^1/_8$", $^3/_{16}$" or $^1/_4$" wide depending upon the tailplane size).
4. Glue a balsa strip along the rear face of the leading edge and the front face of the trailing edge. The size of this strip will depend upon the tailplane thickness – for $^1/_4$" thick tailplanes it will be $^1/_8$" square ($^1/_4$" – 2 × $^1/_{16}$") for $^3/_{16}$" ones it will be $^1/_{16}$" square and so on.

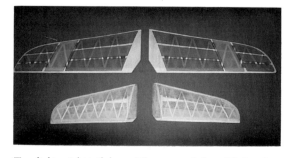

Two lightweight tailplanes. The top one is from **Weekend Warrior** *and weighs 1½ ounces, while the lower one is from Sundancer E400 74" and weighs ¾ ounce.*

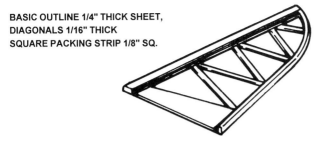

BASIC OUTLINE 1/4" THICK SHEET,
DIAGONALS 1/16" THICK
SQUARE PACKING STRIP 1/8" SQ.

STAGE 1. PIN DOWN T.E., LAMINATED L.E. SHEET AND DIAGONALS
THEN ADD SQUARE STRIP BEHIND L.E. AND IN FRONT OF T.E.

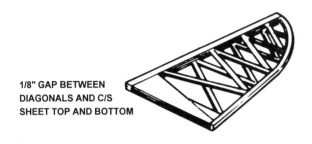

1/8" GAP BETWEEN
DIAGONALS AND C/S
SHEET TOP AND BOTTOM

STAGE 2. ADD TOP SHEETING AND DIAGONALS

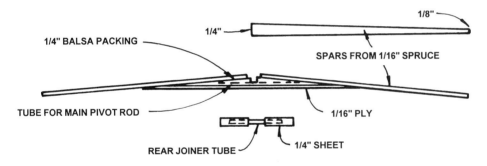

1/4" BALSA PACKING

1/4"

1/8"

SPARS FROM 1/16" SPRUCE

TUBE FOR MAIN PIVOT ROD

1/16" PLY

REAR JOINER TUBE

1/4" SHEET

STAGE 3. ASSEMBLE SPAR/MAIN JOINER TUBE WITH 1/16" PLY BRACE
AND PACKING, ASSEMBLE REAR JOINER WITH 1/4" BALSA

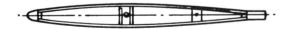

STAGE 4. SLIDE SPAR INTO TAILPLANE HALVES TO PRODUCE SECTION
AS SHOWN. FIX IN PLACE WITH CYANO, INSERT REAR JOINER BLOCK

STAGE 5. SAW THROUGH JOINER TUBES, FIT 1/16" PLY ROOT RIBS.
CARVE L.E. TO SECTION AND SAND

Figure 8.7 *Lightweight anti-warp AMT.*

5. Now add the top layer of diagonals, running in opposition to the bottom layer, and the top centre section sheeting.

6. Cut the spar from spruce sheet ($^1/_8$" for large tailplanes, $^1/_{16}$" for smaller ones – up to 100S soarer size). This depth of the spar at the root is equivalent to the maximum finished tailplane thickness less $^1/_8$". It should taper at the tip to a thickness equivalent to the gap between the top and bottom diagonals.

7. Assemble the spar complete with a one-piece tube to take the main pivot (with the tailplane shape shown which requires some sweep back on the spar this will involve extra balsa structure and thin ply braces so that the tube is at 90 degrees at the root) and also make up a shorter tube for the rear activating pin, set into balsa of the appropriate thickness.

8. Remove the tailplane halves from the plan, mark the spar position in pencil on each top diagonal and slide them onto the spars, thus forcing out the diagonals and root sheeting to produce the desired section. Fit the secondary joiner tube assembly into the root at the same time. When everything is nicely lined up, attach the spar to the root sheeting and diagonals by running in thin cyano adhesive.

9. Saw through the tubes and structure at the centre, cut back the balsa around the tubes and cap the roots with $^1/_{16}$" ply end ribs.

10. Finally, carve and sand the leading and trailing edges to section and lightly sand the tailplanes overall prior to covering. The structure is very stiff and is suitable for all types of covering.

While this assembly sequence may sound complicated, it really is extremely straightforward and tailplanes of this type are very quick to build once the technique is understood. Variations in the structure and insertion of extra reinforcing where required are extremely easy and make the system suitable for all-moving tailplanes of all sizes. For very large or highly stressed applications, the whole structure can be covered in $^1/_{32}$ inch balsa.

The two tailplanes in the photograph are both covered in 5 micron mylar with tissue on top and finished in multi-coloured tissue with three coats of cellulose dope. The all-up weight of the smaller one is 18 grams while the larger one is 40 grams, and both are amply strong in bending and torsionally as stiff as the proverbial surfboard.

Foam tailplanes can use exactly the same structure as a foam cored wing. However, only the lightest foam and covering materials should be used to keep the weight to an acceptable figure. Bare foam tailplanes covered in thin wrapping paper, using a spar to carry the joiner tubes in the case of an all-moving type are satisfactory; they will need to be edged with balsa, the rear component being thick enough to accept the hinges in the case of an elevator tailplane.

Foam/veneer structures are less commonly used for tailplanes, they are only normally found on larger RTF and ARTF models. For this application, sheeting with $^1/_{32}$" balsa is preferable to hardwood veneer in order to minimise weight.

Foam cores with glass cloth skins, often featuring carbon fibre reinforcement laid up on top of the core before the skins are added, is a method which is favoured by many producers of high class competitive RTF models. Given the appropriate moulds in which to 'press' the tailplane while the resin cures, or the use of a vacuum bagging system to apply pressure, components of a very high standard of finish and good strength/weight ratio can be produced, but as with moulded wings, the techniques involved are beyond the scope of all but the skilled and dedicated home builder.

Having considered the flying surfaces, which are really the heart of any R/C glider, we come now to the component whose major functions are to contain the radio equipment and hold the flying surfaces apart at the correct distance from and angle to each other – the fuselage. The foregoing statement may seem to downgrade the importance of this component, and, in truth, what we are looking for is simply an adequately strong structure which will fulfil these requirements while producing the smallest possible amount of drag. However, almost all model fuselages, even those of models designed as purely competitive tools, pay some regard to aesthetic considerations; it is perhaps fortunate that the most efficient aerodynamic forms usually coincide with what most people find to be aesthetically pleasing lines.

It is in the field of fuselage construction that glassfibre has made its biggest inroads into model glider structures, to the extent that moulded shell fuselages in either glassfibre or some other form of plastic can now be considered to be the most commonplace form found on any flying field. However, popular as the glassfibre shell fuselage is, it is far from being the only, or, in specific instances, even the best alternative. The usual options are:

- Full fibreglass shell fuselage, often including fin moulding.
- Fibreglass pod mated to separate fibreglass boom.
- Balsa/ply full fuselage.
- Rolled ply full fuselage.
- Balsa and ply pod mated to glass fibre boom.
- For special applications, usually PSS slope models, balsa box structure padded out to section with hot-wire cut foam 'cheeks', and

covered in either brown paper, self-adhesive masking tape or computer paper, finished with varnish. In this way, complex fuselage sections such as are often found on the modern jet aircraft which are such popular PSS subjects can be reproduced.

The method of producing a full fibreglass shell fuselage, while not especially difficult is time consuming and rather messy. The other problem is that, due to the amount of work involved in preparing the initial pattern and moulds, one has to be really sure that the fuselage dimensions will be correct. This type of fuselage only really makes sense if the intention is to produce a large number of duplicates, probably on a commercial or semi-commercial basis.

The technique involves first producing a pattern or 'plug' of the finished fuselage. Professional mouldmakers carve these from suitable wood, but as a less artistic alternative, a pattern can be built up from balsa and foam. The problem with this latter approach is in getting the required standard of finish on the plug; in order to produce a top class finish on the final fuselage shell, the finish on the pattern must also be top class. Once the pattern is prepared, a heavy female mould is made from it, in two halves. This is normally made from chopped strand glassfibre mat, and must be thick and rigid to obviate any chance of it warping.

Once the female moulds are ready, the final fuselages are laid up in them, and either joined while still in the moulds or after they have cured

My 140 inch **Weekend Warrior** *open class thermal soarer has glassfibre pod and boom structure.*

and been trimmed and removed. Either relatively cheap polyester resin (the type sold in car body repair kits) or the more resilient and expensive epoxy resin can be used for the lay-up, and materials ranging from cheap chopped strand mat to sophisticated kevlar and carbon fibre can be used. Naturally, when buying a commercial fuselage, the cost of the finished item tends to reflect the cost of the material used in the lay-up. As with most things in life, what at first seems to be a bargain may be found to be wanting in the areas of strength and weight distribution.

One way of checking a fibreglass shell fuselage, apart from examining the standard of finish and establishing what type of material has been used in the lay-up, is to check the longitudinal balance point. Any bare shell that balances aft of the wing trailing edge position should be viewed with reservations, as the finished model will probably require excessive amounts of nose ballast.

Most clubs have members who produce a few fibreglass fuselages, either for sale to clubmates or among local modellers by word of mouth, and this is perhaps the best way to obtain a fibreglass shell fuselage for that new model. In addition there are a number of semi-commercial cottage industries who offer mouldings, and, of course, most RTF and ARTF models use fuselages of this type, as well as a large number of conventional kit models.

The same comments also apply to the two-part fibreglass fuselage, which is simpler to mould by virtue of the fact that the tailboom is a separate tubular fibreglass section, usually a fishing rod section, which is plugged onto (or into) the front pod shell moulding. Because of the way in which these rod mouldings are produced, quite light but rigid seamless tubes result, which means that it is much easier to get a good weight distribution with this type than with the full moulded fuselage.

Whatever style of fibreglass shell is used, a certain amount of internal structure to accept wing mounting dowels, towhook, radio gear etc. will be required. Reinforcement of open edges (e.g. hatch openings) by hardwood strips may also be required. Bonding wooden parts to epoxy moulded fuselages is quite easy, since most epoxy adhesives will work well. However, it can be much more difficult with polyester resin, and very tricky indeed with some of the kit model thermoplastic mouldings. For polyester resin, structural members have to be coated with the same resin, and as this is not really an adhesive, reinforced with glass cloth and resin. Some types of instant cyano adhesive work, but only if the fits of the parts are very good – and since the inside of a moulded fuselage has, in contrast to the outside, a quite rough finish, this can be difficult to achieve. Non-structural internal fittings, such as those used for radio gear mounting, can be fitted in place using silicon sealant.

If we consider the advantages of the glassfibre shell fuselage, these might be listed as convenience and speed of building, ease with which a well streamlined aerodynamic shape might be produced and, depending upon the circumstances, ready availability of a spare. The disadvantages are, however, equally obvious; difficulty in fitting radio equipment into a complete shell (it is much easier if provision for mounting components can be built in during assembly), cost, possible poor weight distribution and difficulty of repair. I have no hesitation in stating that a properly designed wooden fuselage can be both more resistant to damage, and much easier to repair if it is damaged than the equivalent fibreglass shell. For this reason, unless going down the RTF route, the newcomer is strongly recommended to start with a wooden fuselage.

Constructing a wooden fuselage for a soaring model is not difficult. If the model is a beginner's type, where ultimate performance and appearance take second place to ease of construction, strength and ease of repair, then a simple rectangular box of balsa sheet, with ply doublers to reinforce the nose area and spruce longerons ($1/8$"

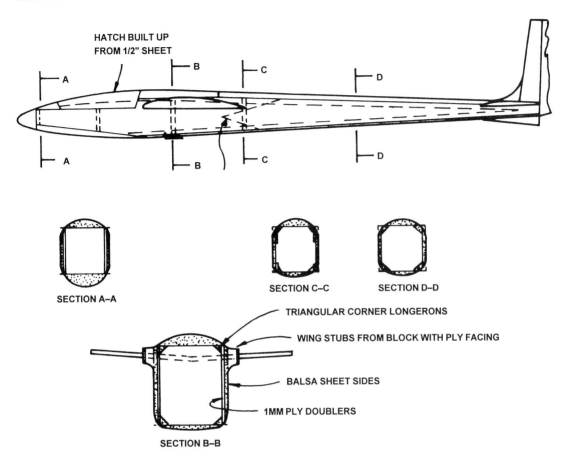

Figure 8.8 *Balsa box fuselage structure.*

square is usually adequate) in all four corners will serve very well. It is also easy to build the fin into this kind of fuselage, merely trapping it between the rear fuselage sides and reinforcing the fitting as required. As can be seen by the illustration in Figure 8.8, quite a streamlined structure can be produced if triangular section balsa longerons are substituted for the spruce to permit the corners to be carved away.

A development of this simplest of structures can be used to produce a fuselage of good aerodynamic form and outstanding strength. In this case the basic fuselage is built as a box with spruce corner longerons, as described above, but the cross section is restricted to the absolute minimum to hold the radio equipment – it is literally designed around the battery, Rx and servos. The outside of this box is then clad in the softest available balsa sheet – $1/8$" thick top bottom and sides aft of the wing trailing edge, $1/4$" sides and $3/8$" top and bottom forward of this. The fuselage can then be carved and sanded to an aesthetically pleasant and aerodynamically efficient shape, following which it is clad in lightweight (1 ounce per square metre) glass cloth and epoxy skinning resin, with two layers of cloth in high stress areas such as the lower nose and wing mount. A final coat of resin and sanding with wet and dry paper will produce

61

Tail of my **Metre Maid** *two metre model showing removable knuckle-hinged rudder and plug-on all-moving tailplane.*

a shape and finish equivalent to a glass shell fuselage, but, as the cross section is a tube with finite wall thickness, with the ply as the inside skin and the glass as the outside, the overall strength will be vastly greater than any glassfibre shell.

As proof of this, the *Metre Maid* two metre soarer shown in the photograph, which uses this kind of fuselage, was buried up to the rear of the

wing in none too soft ground due to a radio failure, and, apart from leaving the nose block behind at the bottom of the fourteen inch hole, the fuselage suffered no damage of any sort.

An alternative way of producing a wooden fuselage of good aerodynamic form is to use the rolled ply type of construction, a schematic of which is shown in Figure 8.9. In this version of the construction a spruce crutch and balsa bottom pan is used, but it is perfectly possible to produce a fuselage that is ply all the way round; if soaked in water, 0.8 mm ply will go round the sharpest curves. However, compound curves are not possible, so some thought to the design layout around the nose area is necessary. There are actually a number of full-size sailplanes, usually the later wooden types, which lend themselves very well as scale models to this form of construction.

Before leaving the wooden fuselage, for thermal soarers and electric soarers in particular, a pod fabricated from balsa and ply, teamed with a fibreglass tube tailboom offers a very sound and relatively simple structure. The pod permits the radio equipment to be built in neatly, while the

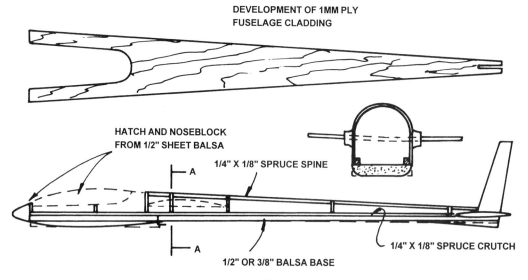

Figure 8.9 *Rolled ply fuselage.*

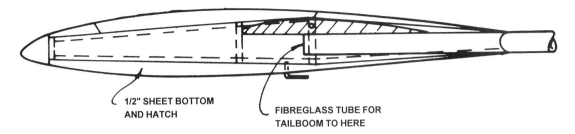

1/2" SHEET BOTTOM
AND HATCH

FIBREGLASS TUBE FOR
TAILBOOM TO HERE

Figure 8.10 *Balsa pod for plug-in wings.*

glass tailboom offers excellent strength/weight ratio in this area. The illustration in Figure 8.10 shows how such a structure might look.

The balsa box/foam fairing structure used on many PSS models is really simply a variation of the ply/balsa/glass fuselage described above, but by restricting the box to the smallest and simplest structure, the foam fairings can be used to produce any shape, no matter how complex. The foam sections are usually cut to shape with a hot wire cutting bow, a smaller version of the type used for foam wing cores, but as some sanding will inevitably be necessary to produce the final shape, blue foam is used rather than white, which is very difficult to sand. Once the final shape is produced, the fuselage can be covered with either self-adhesive parcel tape or thin wrapping paper, or computer listing paper, applied with thinned PVA adhesive. Since the cross section is usually fairly complex, covering has to take place in small strips or sections to accommodate the compound curves. Varnishing with polyurethane, and rubbing down, then spraying with primer and paint can produce an amazingly good finish on this type of fuselage. As

an alternative tougher but heavier covering, glass cloth and epoxy resin (not polyester, as this will attack the foam) can be used, but this is rarely employed on the type of PSS slope models for which the technique is particularly applicable.

This run down on construction techniques is not meant to be comprehensive – a whole book could be devoted to the subject of all the possible variations. However, it can be appreciated that a large range of structural types can be found in soaring models, and the newcomer will quickly develop a liking for one or other of the techniques. Some modellers never build anything but foam cored wing models with moulded glass fuselages, while others specialise entirely in traditional built-up structures. With the exception of the very lightweight models, where nothing beats the open-frame free-flight type structure, and the sophisticated contest machines and large scale models of hi-tech full-size sailplanes, where moulded structures and GRP resins dominate, almost anything can be built by almost any method, and still turn out to be a perfectly satisfactory flying machine. Don't be afraid to experiment!

CHAPTER 9

Control considerations

Even if the newcomer starts off his radio gliding career with an RTF model, one constructional skill which he will need to master is that of installing radio equipment. Depending upon the degree of completeness of the model he may also need to learn how to install control linkages and surface actuating horns, hinge control surfaces and set up controls with the correct amount of movement.

There are three main radio components to mount in the model; the receiver, the receiver battery pack and the servos. The first two of these should pose no problem, as all that is required is that they be wrapped in some shock absorbing foam rubber sheet and positioned as convenient in the model. The normal practice is to position the heaviest component, the Rx battery pack, as far forward in the nose as possible. This has two benefits – it gets the maximum amount of nose weight as far in front of the CG as possible (gliders invariably need to carry nose ballast), and, in the event of a crash, there is no delicate electronic equipment in front of the battery for it to squash!

The next heaviest radio components are the servos, one of which is required for each control function. Logically these should be positioned

next, behind the Rx battery, with the Rx itself behind them. This layout is often used, but can be slightly inconvenient as it means that the Rx has to be positioned under the control runs from the servos. For this reason, one often sees the Rx mounted between the battery pack and the servos – either layout is perfectly acceptable, although the first offers the best weight distribution and crash protection. Unlike the Rx and battery, the servos, as they must exert mechanical force, need to be mechanically attached to the airframe. To facilitate this, servos are provided with mounting lugs into which rubber grommets are fitted so that the servo may be mounted with two or four self-tapping screws onto appropriately spaced hardwood (ply or spruce) mounts. Many radio outfits are supplied with pre-moulded plastic trays to take two or three servos, and while these can be used in some applications (notably in power models), it will be found that the majority of sailplane fuselages are too slim to permit their use. However, one advantage which gliders and electric models have is that there is no vibration present (or a very minimal amount in the case of an electric model). In a power model the servos must be soft mounted using the rubber grommets to isolate them as much as possible from vibra-

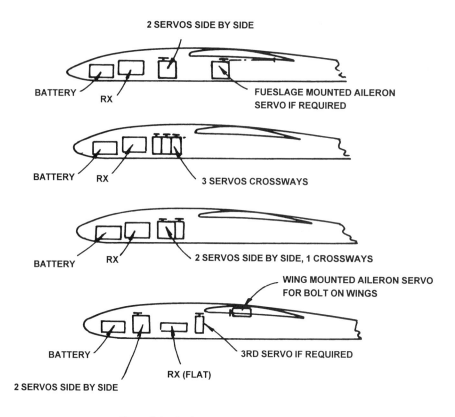

Figure 9.1 *Radio equipment disposition.*

tion which will eventually damage them. In a glider we can, if we wish, hard mount the servos, although many people do still use the grommets to provide some level of protection from shock loads.

The outlines in Figure 9.1 show schematics of various options for equipment layout for rudder/ elevator and rudder/elevator/aileron models. For the actual mounting of the servos, some forethought is required, either when building the

Installation of two Futaba mini servos in vintage Jader 60. Note the elevator idler crank system and closed-loop rudder cables.

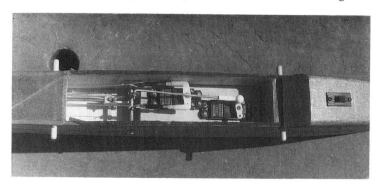

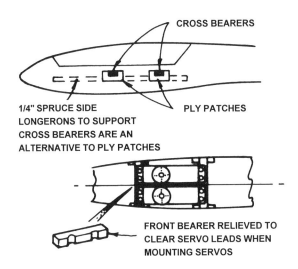

1/4" SPRUCE SIDE
LONGERONS TO SUPPORT
CROSS BEARERS ARE AN
ALTERNATIVE TO PLY PATCHES

CROSS BEARERS

PLY PATCHES

FRONT BEARER RELIEVED TO
CLEAR SERVO LEADS WHEN
MOUNTING SERVOS

Figure 9.2 *Servos mounted on cross rails.*

fuselage in wood or in the early stages of fitting out a glassfibre or plastic shell fuselage, to incorporate suitable rails or supports so that the cross rails to mount the servos can be fitted later – refer to Figure 9.2. If there is sufficient space, the servos can be mounted in a ply tray and this can be screwed to hardwood side rails, making insertion and removal of the servos for servicing easier.

Other matters to consider when installing the radio are the positioning of the on/off switch and the receiver aerial. Typically on/off switches are of the simple slide variety, and can be fitted so that the toggle protrudes through the fuselage side for operation (fit it so that the ON position is towards the back, so that if it should accidentally be caught during launching the radio will not be switched off – a point born of bitter experience!). There is no problem in fitting a switch this way in a glider, since, unlike a power model installation, it will not be subjected to oily exhaust residue, however, some modellers prefer to install the switch internally, mounted either on the front of the servo tray or independently. In such cases, either the hatch is removed to operate the switch, or a short pushrod is fabricated to protrude through the fuselage side, with a threaded end which is screwed into the switch toggle. Once again, to guard against accidental switching off, the push direction should be ON.

Normally aerials are run down light plastic tubes installed in the fuselage; in smaller models where the aerial length is greater than the available fuselage distance, the tube exits at the rear

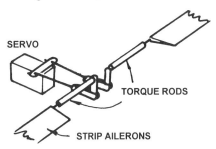

SERVO

TORQUE RODS

STRIP AILERONS

Figure 9.3 *Fuselage mounted servo driving strip ailerons.*

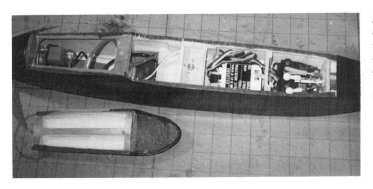

*Simple installation in **Sundancer 60** E400 electric soarer has Hitec mini servos for rudder and all-moving tailplanes at extreme right, next is the Micro 6 receiver and then a long gap with power battery below to RSC210 electronic on/off switch mounted on the back of the motor.*

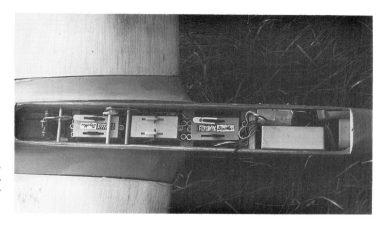

Three servos in this slim fuselage; the front one is for air brakes while the other two drive a mechanical mixer for the 'V' tail (mixer behind rearmost servo).

and the extra aerial length is allowed to trail behind the model. Rx aerials should *never* be shortened to fit them within an airframe, as loss of range will result. One other warning – do not run an aerial down the inside of a carbon-fibre tail boom, or a carbon-fibre reinforced glassfibre fuselage, or loss of radio contact may be experienced in certain attitudes. In such cases, the aerial is better run up to the fin, or if this would present too much drag, then a tube installed in the wing can be used; whatever method is adopted the aerial wire should not be in the same plane as any longitudinal carbon-fibre reinforcements.

On aileron equipped models there are basically four options for the installation of the aileron servo. The first, really only suitable for smaller slope soaring models, is to mount the servo in the fuselage and drive the ailerons via a pair of pushrods, which must be detached each time the wing is removed. The second option, which is similar in operation but eliminates the need to disconnect the aileron horns, is to mount the servo in the wing centre section, protruding down into the fuselage, and drive the ailerons via a pair of pushrods connected to horns on the end of torque rods. Alternatively, the servo can be mounted flat, on its side, in the wing centre section and the drive taken either via two tube-in-tube control snakes or pushrods and ninety-degree cranks. The final, and easiest solution, is

to mount a small (mini size for larger models, micro for smaller ones) servo some distance outboard in each wing and drive the ailerons via individual pushrods. The two servos will need to be connected to one Rx output using a 'Y' lead, an accessory which is available for most radio outfits. If using a computer transmitter, the servos may each be connected to one output and mixed so that aileron and flap action are available from the one control surface. Figures 9.3, 9.4 and 9.5 illustrate the variations.

Once the servos are mounted in the model, they must be connected to actuate the control surface. The three most popular ways of doing this are by using either a plastic tube-in-tube commercial snake, a hardwood dowel or hard balsa pushrod, or closed-loop cables made from nylon coated wire sold in angling shops as fishing trace wire.

If it is decided to use snakes – a thin plastic tube sliding within a close fitting plastic outer tube – there are a couple of points to bear in mind. First, it is false economy to use the cheapest snakes; be prepared to pay for the best ones which give the smoothest operation. Secondly, no matter how good the snake is, if there are severe bends in the control run, control slop problems may arise, so try to keep the control runs absolutely straight. Thirdly, the length of inner tube exposed at each end should be kept to the

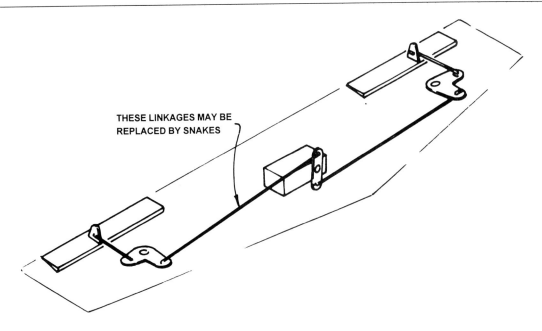

THESE LINKAGES MAY BE
REPLACED BY SNAKES

Figure 9.4   *Single wing mounted servo driving outboard ailerons.*

'MINI' SERVO

ACCESS HATCH

CROSS SECTION OF WING
AT SERVO POSITION

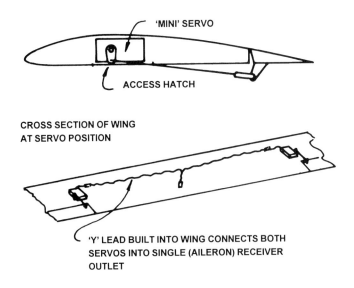

'Y' LEAD BUILT INTO WING CONNECTS BOTH
SERVOS INTO SINGLE (AILERON) RECEIVER
OUTLET

Figure 9.5   *Separate mini servo in each wing for aileron drive.*

69

This photograph of a neat standard class model shows the normal front to rear installation sequence in a glider – Rx battery, then Rx and finally servos.

absolute minimum necessary to accommodate the required control movement – an exposed snake inner is subject to bending and flexing under stress, thus losing control movement when air pressure is present on the control surface. Fourthly, also to avoid loss of surface movement, the snake outer must be firmly anchored to the airframe, as a minimum at the front and back, and preferably at several points in between. This can be achieved with cyano adhesive, or by wrapping the tube in masking tape and using epoxy adhesive, or by the use of small plastic saddle clamps (but if using these make sure that the outer tube is not squashed causing friction in the control run).

Carefully and properly fitted good quality snakes are a very satisfactory method of control surface actuation on almost all models – badly fitted or poor quality snakes can be a control nightmare, introducing slop and friction into the system which will lead to wandering control surface neutrals and poor control response. With regard to the end fittings for connection to the servo output arm and control surface control horn, most snakes are provided with screw-in rods onto which a forked metal or plastic clevis can then be screwed, to give an end coupling which will permit a degree of length adjustment once installed. Sometimes a simple, non-adjustable wire connector is used at one end, with an adjustable one at the other.

Pushrods, other than the short ones used between aileron surfaces and servos, cannot be made from wire due to lack of stiffness and excess weight. Longer pushrods, running from the rudder and elevator servos right to the tail of the model need to be either hardwood dowel (¼ inch diameter minimum) or ³/₈" square hard balsa, with wire end fittings bound and epoxied to each end. A better, if more expensive, alternative is to use carbon-fibre arrow shafts which are unmatched for stiffness/weight ratio. Remember, in this case though, not to run the aerial down the tailboom in company with the carbon pushrods, or loss of radio control may result in certain attitudes. End connections use the same clevises as described above, screwed direct onto the threaded ends of the wire which is fitted to the pushrods. As with snakes, every effort should be made to keep the control run between servo arm and surface horn in a straight line – Figure 9.6 illustrates the kind of installation to avoid.

Wire closed-loop connections rely upon a tensioned trace wire running from each side of a double-ended servo arm to horns each side of the control surface – the principle is illustrated in Figure 9.7. Simple to install in the case of a rudder (which is the surface for which it is most frequently used), some special mechanics are involved in order to use this system on an all-moving tailplane, one way of achieving this is shown in Figure 9.8. This set-up works very well if carefully installed.

One general point to remember in all installations is that slop of control surfaces i.e the ability of the control surface to move without the servo moving, is the great enemy of precise control. Excess slop can promote a situation where the control surface does not neutralise exactly, causing the flight of the model to wander unpredictably – bad if the surface is rudder, worse in the case of ailerons and potentially disastrous if it happens to the elevator or all-moving tail control. In extreme cases loose surfaces can start up flutter as the speed of the model increases lead-

WRONG! STEEP BEND LIKE THIS ALLOWS
FLEXING, CAUSES SURFACE 'BLOW BACK'

Figure 9.6　*Incorrect pushrod geometry.*

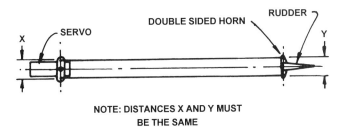

NOTE: DISTANCES X AND Y MUST
BE THE SAME

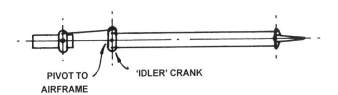

Figure 9.7　*Basic closed-loop control link.*

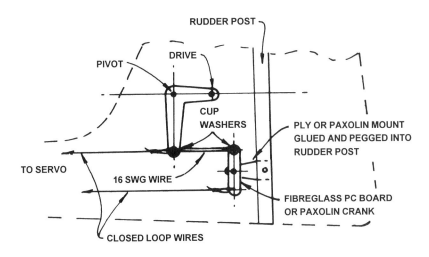

Figure 9.8　*Method of using closed-loop drive for all-moving tailplane.*

ing to ultimate structural failure of either the control surface hinges or the whole model. The key to avoiding slop in control surfaces is to keep all control runs straight and make sure that all holes in servo arms and control surface horns are *exact* fits on the pin of the clevis on the control rod. Excess clearance fits simply will not do.

Before leaving control surface connection, just a word about 'V' tails. This type of tail is popular on both thermal and slope soarers. In the latter case, the rudder action is sometimes dispensed with, which means that the elevators are simply driven up and down from one servo via some form of forked connector on the end of the pushrod or snake. However, if the surfaces

are to provide both pitch and yaw (elevator and rudder) control, then some form of **mixer** is required. If a computer transmitter is being used, this mixing can be carried out at the transmitter, and in the model all that is required is that one servo should be connected to each side of the V tail. However, there are a number of mechanical options to permit a non-computer radio to operate the V tail control surfaces in both senses i.e. to operate them as ruddervators. The simplest of these to understand and install is the sliding servo as illustrated in Figure 9.9, where the elevator servo drives the rudder servo back and forth on a tray which slides on wire rails – a highly effective solution providing all tolerances

(A)

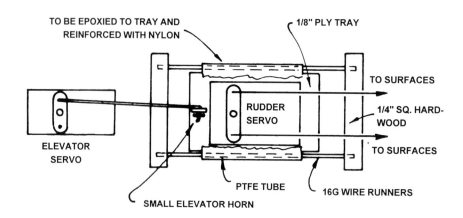

(B)

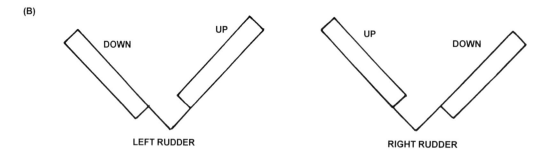

Figure 9.9 (a) Sliding servo mixer; (b) 'V' tail rudder action viewed from rear.

are kept close to eliminate slop. It is also worth emphasising that the required rudder control movement on a V tail is in the same sense as a rudder, not like ailerons. In other words, when viewed from the rear, for a left turn, the left-hand surface will go *down* and the right-hand surface *up*.

Finally, what are the options for hinging the control surfaces? The most popular and commonly seen method is to insert small pieces of thin mylar material in slots cut on the centre-line of the surface (in a thickness sense). These hinges are pegged securely to the mounting surface and control surface by drilling $1/16''$ dia. metre holes and fitting small lengths of wooden cocktail stick secured with cyano instant glue. The hinging action then bends the mylar, and provided that maximum control surface deflection required is no more than about 30 degrees, the degree of stiffness present is quite acceptable. As an alternative there are many commercial hinges available which consist of moulded halves with metal hinge pins inserted. These are inserted in much the same way as the mylar ones described above, but care is required to keep the glue used clear of the hinge pin.

Surfaces can be hinged using self-adhesive tape (not ordinary transparent tape, which is not weatherproof, but the special tape produced for joining transparent plastic roofing sheets) or plastic covering film – the sequence of achieving this on an aileron hinge is shown in Figure 9.10. An advantage of this method is that the gap between the surfaces is sealed, which both reduces drag and improves control effectiveness.

Whatever hinging method is used, the main two considerations must be freedom of movement – stiff hinges cause servos to be constantly hunting and consume power, reducing the duration obtained from the Rx battery and also preventing surfaces from neutralising properly – and closeness of fit to minimise gaps. Figure 9.11 shows a simple way in which a thin strip of plastic foam, draught excluder tape is suitable, can be

used to seal the hinge gap when mylar or plastic pinned hinges are used.

On the subject of control surface deflection; any reputable RTF, ARTF, kit or plan should

(A) JOIN TWO STRIPS OF TAPE

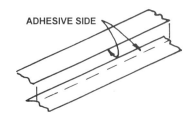

(B) CUT TAPE INTO 1/2" SLICES

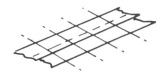

(C) APPLY SLICES TO WING

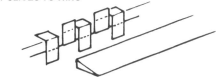

(D) FIT AILERON

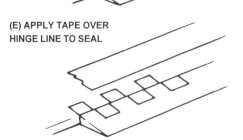

(E) APPLY TAPE OVER HINGE LINE TO SEAL

Figure 9.10   *Tape hinging aileron.*

73

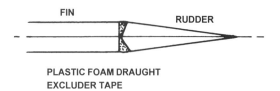

Figure 9.11 *Hinge gap sealing.*

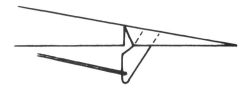

(A) AILERON HORN – NO DIFFERENTIAL

(B) AILERON HORN TO GIVE DIFFERENTIAL

Figure 9.12 *Horn geometry for differential.*

include information on the recommended deflection for the control surfaces. For the beginner the advice would be to use a little more than the full amount recommended for the rudder, rather less than the quoted level for the elevator or all-moving tailplane and precisely what is recommended for the ailerons, if fitted. One other thing to consider with aileron controls is the subject of differential movement. Due to the fact that the downgoing aileron (the one on the outside of the turn, lifting the wing) generates drag as well as extra lift for that wing, whereas the upgoing one generates very little extra drag. The result of this, if both upgoing and downgoing ailerons move through the same angle, is that right aileron will cause the model to bank to the right, but the higher drag produced by the downgoing (left) aileron may also cause it to yaw to the left, thus making it very difficult to fly precisely. The higher the aspect ratio of the wing (and gliders are usually high aspect ratio aircraft) the more pronounced this effect is.

In order to reduce or eliminate the problem of adverse yaw, it is normal to incorporate differential movement – less aileron down movement than up – on almost all R/C sailplanes which use ailerons except low aspect ratio slope aerobatic

models. The amount of differential required varies, some of the very high aspect ratio thermal soaring models and scale gliders require as much as three to one differential i.e. the upgoing aileron moves through three times the angle of the downgoing one. The most usual way to achieve the required differential is by adjusting the control horn geometry – Figure 9.12 compares the normally mounted horn for equal up and down movement as used on an elevator, and an aileron horn mounted so that the pushrod connection is behind the hinge line which will result in the desired differential movement. Once again, life is slightly easier with the more sophisticated computer radios as many of these permit differential amounts of movement to be programmed into all the main control channels.

CHAPTER 10

Covering and finishing

Unless the newcomer is going to go the complete ready-to-fly route, decisions will need to be made about the type of finish which is to be applied to the model. The broad categories available are:

- Covering in tissue, silk or nylon with a finish of cellulose shrinking dope applied – the 'traditional' modelling method as used on model aircraft for the last 60 or more years. However, there are one or two recent developments in this type of finish which will be described.
- Use of a plastic film covering ready coated with heat-sensitive adhesive.
- Woven fabric covering with heat-sensitive adhesive
- Epoxy resin/glasscloth finish, either applied freehand and rubbed down or vacuum bagged onto the surface to produce a completed finish.

There are minor variations; for example, some lightweight plastic film coverings are available without adhesive, in order to save weight. In this case a suitable heat-sensitive adhesive has to be brushed onto the appropriate parts of the airframe.

Probably the most popular and commonly encountered type of finish is the heat-shrink plastic film. The reasons for its popularity are not difficult to discern; it is relatively economical in that the film represents the complete finish, there

Nice example of translucent plastic film finish on Brian Lord's **Gentle Lady** *lightweight two metre model. The fuselage is also finished in film; this time opaque.*

being no extras to purchase (although, for best results, suitable application tools are required, usually a special electric iron and a heat gun). It also has a high surface finish, is quick and reasonably easy to apply and the various films are available in a vast range of colours, with both translucent and solid effects, and, unlike the use of some dopes and resins, no noxious fumes are created during the covering process. What then are the drawbacks which prevent film being used in all applications? There are two principal problems; the first, that of edges of film lifting and general lack of durability of the finish is not so important on gliders and electric models as, unlike IC powered aircraft, fuel residue seepage will not be a problem. The second drawback, however, can be serious, especially on lighter sailplanes which rely on the covering to provide a type of 'stressed skin' to the structure, adding torsional rigidity. Films are very poor in this respect. Thus, while films are excellent general purpose finishes for models such as foam winged slope and thermal soarers and stronger built-up models, they do leave something to be desired on such lightweights as HLGs and electric soarers, unless great care is taken to produce a structure which does not rely on the covering to any great degree for its torsional strength.

Once the basic technique is mastered, applying a film finish is a quick and easy job. However, there is a world of difference between the best and worst results seen, and it is necessary to stress that the quality of the finished model, not withstanding the excellent surface finish of the film itself, will depend to a very great extent on the quality of finish of the underlying airframe. Indeed, film can cause problems here, as due to its high gloss any little bumps and pits on the surface will be emphasised. The general technique of application is much the same for all the various films on the market; some require slightly different temperature settings on the electric iron to produce optimum results however, and most types of film are supplied with an instruction leaflet which contains much useful advice.

The first step in film covering is to prepare the structure. It is perfectly possible to cover onto bare balsa but it is much easier to get a smooth and even surface if the balsa is first treated with two or three coats of either sanding sealer or cellulose dope, sanding gently after each coat is dry. Any obvious holes or pits should be filled with a suitable filler at this stage, and sanded smooth. Before starting to film cover it is now most important to remove all balsa dust from the model structure and the working area. A vacuum cleaner is useful here, but a final wipe over of the airframe with one of the special 'tack rags' sold in car accessory shops for use in car spraying is the best way to ensure that no dust will be trapped under the film. Remember that the film will probably have a static electric build-up on it which will positively attract dust, so do not skip these preparations.

There are products available from film manufacturers which, if used in difficult areas of the airframe, will ensure better adhesion of the film; these are essentially additional heat-sensitive adhesives that are brushed on and allowed to dry, to be re-activated when the film is applied. It is well worth using these compounds in areas where joins will occur in the film to ensure that the edges will not lift after a little use.

After the piece of film has been cut to shape, allowing a suitable overlap all round, a portion of the backing sheet is peeled away at one end and the film is tacked in place with a warm iron. The remainder of the backing is progressively peeled off as the film is gently stretched and tacked in place. The aim at this stage is not drum tightness – ample shrinkage is available later – but rather to get a smooth and even cover with no wrinkles or creases. Film can, with care, be worked around quite severe compound curves without cutting. The trick is to stretch it and iron it down a little at a time, working slowly and carefully. Using this technique, a demonstrator from one of the film manufacturers can actually film cover one hemisphere of a four inch diameter ball without any cutting or creases at all, but few modellers are that good! However, with care, the average wing tip or compound curved fuselage nose area can easily be handled. One problem that many people experience is that of the filming iron bruising the soft balsa surface, and leaving indentations which show clearly through the film. A good way of minimising this difficulty is to use a sock of suitable material over the sole of the iron, adjusting the heat up slightly to compensate. It is also worth noting that a balsa surface which has been treated with a couple of coats of cellulose clear dope or sanding sealer is less prone to damage in this way than is bare balsa.

Once all the covering for the surface has been tacked in place, it can be properly attached around the edges and onto intermediate points such as rib capstrips etc.; again, great care is required not to iron-in wrinkles at this stage. Some modellers only iron the film onto the extreme outline of the component, relying on the subsequent shrinking to attach it to the rest of the airframe. While this may well give the best finish, it can be somewhat suspect in terms of strength as the covering is not necessarily firmly attached to, say, each rib on a wing.

Once the whole of a surface has been covered, and the overlaps at the edges ironed over, the film can be shrunk using the heatgun. When covering the opposite surface, areas where film overlaps onto film should be treated with a coat of heat-sensitive adhesive prior to ironing the overlap down, to ensure that it will not lift in future. Poorly attached film can be a positive hazard; on more than one occasion I have seen the whole covering of one surface of a wing panel strip off in flight when a section of the film overlap at the leading edge has lifted, much to the detriment of the sailplane's flying performance!

Extra decoration cut from contrasting colour film can be ironed in place on top of the basic finish, once again the use of one of the additional adhesives marketed by the manufacturers is strongly recommended to stop this from lifting. Alternatively, smaller sheets of strongly self-adhesive trim film are available in matching colours and are ideal for producing letters and motifs.

As previously stated, a well executed film finish can look really good, the main points to remember are:

1. Be sure that the airframe (in particular the flying surfaces) has sufficient inherent torsional rigidity to not have to rely on the film for this.
2. Read the manufacturer's instructions.
3. Take great care to obtain a smooth, even finish on the bare airframe.
4. Clean the prepared airframe and work area to remove all dust before starting.
5. Take your time, work carefully and don't be afraid to use the iron to soften adhesive and reposition film to eliminate creases.
6. Treat all overlaps with an additional heat-sensitive adhesive, and with a coat of clear lacquer after completion.

The greater part of the weight of a film finish is not in the actual film material itself, but in the coating of heat-sensitive adhesive which provides both the adhesion to the airframe and the colour of the film. For lightweight models, in particular HLGs and electric soarers, a significant weight saving can be obtained by using one of the several types of film-like products on the market which do not have a coating of adhesive. With these products the adhesive is applied, with a small brush, only to those parts of the airframe where it is required, and after it has dried completely, the covering is attached in exactly the same way as described above, using the iron to re-activate the adhesive. A further extension of this technique, marrying mylar covering with traditional model tissue and cellulose dope finishing is described later.

For larger models, and those requiring a finish more durable than the normal film, a range of heat-shrink fabrics is available. These come in a vast range of finishes, but caution is required as some of the more opaque and/or glossy ones can be quite heavy. These types of covering can also exercise a very strong pull indeed on the airframe when shrunk, so their use should be restricted to models which are of adequate size to carry the weight involved and strongly enough built to cope with the stresses imposed by the covering. The heat-shrink fabric gives a particularly good representation of the type of finish found on full-size gliders of the pre-fibreglass era, and for this reason is much favoured for the beautiful large scale sailplanes which some modellers create. It is also suitable for use on knockabout slope soaring models and on larger thermal soaring types.

Application of heat-shrink fabric coverings is little different from that of films, except that somewhat higher temperatures may be required, and it will be found that some types are not as easy to work around compound curves as film, although this is still possible with care.

Without doubt, one of the most satisfactory and durable finishes for solid surfaces – fuselages, sheet covered built-up wings or foam/veneer wings – is glasscloth and epoxy resin. However, before the modeller embarks on such a finish, a few drawbacks should be considered. Firstly, resin is messy to work with, and the very thin glasscloth required (20–40 grams per square metre) in order to keep the weight of the finish within bounds is difficult to handle. Secondly, unless some form of mould or vacuum bagging system is used, which is normally outside the scope of the average enthusiast, producing the final finish to the very high standards possible with glass/resin is going to require a great deal of hard work with wet and dry abrasive paper. Finally, while providing great additional torsional strength, and excellent resistance to knocks, epoxy/glass is never going to be a particularly light finish, especially as it is basically a natural finish, so that, if

Heat-shrink tissue used on this simple electric soarer in bold, straightforward colour scheme (red/yellow).

colour is required, there will be an additional weight penalty for sprayed or brushed-on paint.

The use of moulds and vacuum bagging is outside the scope of this book, but if the modeller wishes to experiment with a simple epoxy/glass finish, then it is recommended that he tries it on something like a small to medium sized slope aerobatic model to get a feel for the technique before tackling something more ambitious such as a cross-country model or large thermal soarer. A word or two of caution. It is possible to become sensitised to epoxy resin if using it in

Natural epoxy glass finish with sprayed decoration on this thermal soarer.

substantial quantities, with all sorts of subsequent unpleasant skin and breathing problems. Take sensible precautions; work in a well ventilated area, use a barrier cream and disposable gloves and wear a fume mask. Epoxy resins do not have an overtly unpleasant odour, but that does not mean they can be treated in a cavalier fashion, like most chemicals, if mishandled they can cause problems.

As for all coverings, surface preparation is important; make sure that all hollows are filled and all bumps removed and that the overall finish is sanded smooth, and then remove all dust from the airframe and the work area. It is particularly important with epoxy resin covering to have all the tools and materials to hand when you start, and to keep the work area clean and tidy. Cut a piece of glasscloth to size with at least one inch of overlap all round. This glasscloth is very difficult to cut neatly; a good tip here is to lay masking tape on the cloth along the cutting lines and then, using sharp scissors, cut down the middle of the tape. Do not attempt to do too much at once; in any case wings will have to be done one surface at a time, and the most it is prudent to try to complete in one session is both top surfaces of the wing or both bottom surfaces. It is also important that the work area is at a reasonable temperature, not less than 65 degrees, to ensure that the resin will mix and flow smoothly, and cure properly – this is not a job to undertake in a garage in the middle of January!

Once the cloth is prepared, mix the resin carefully strictly in accordance with the instructions, mixing only enough for the area to be immediately covered. It is a great help to just tack the cloth in place at one end with three or four tiny spots of cyano adhesive. Load the brush with resin (you will need a supply of cheap but reliable brushes – you do not want ones which shed hairs all over, but unless you take great care to wash them out in thinners, then soap and water **immediately** after use, they will be ruined) and brush a line down the length of the surface e.g. for a wing

top surface, along the high point of the wing section. Now work outwards, wetting up the cloth thoroughly, but working the resin in and avoiding excess resin – make it go as far as you can. Once the whole of the area is resined, it is now most important to remove as much of the excess as possible, in order to avoid weight build-up. The two usual techniques for this are to either blot the surface with a paper (kitchen) towel roll, or to scrape the excess resin to the edges using a flexible steel straightedge. It is at this stage where the disposable gloves will be very much appreciated, the resin tends to get everywhere and it is very sticky.

The resin must now be left to cure to a 'green' stage i.e. firm but not yet hard, at which point the overlaps should be trimmed off with a very sharp scalpel. It is not wise to attempt to wrap cloth around wing leading edges etc., as this will almost inevitably result in bubbles and lifting of the cloth. The usual method for finishing edges is to use a plain bead of resin. The other surfaces of the component can be tackled at this stage, as the existing resin will be dry enough for limited handling.

Once the whole component is covered, it must be left to cure thoroughly; a little *gentle* heat helps here, but do not overdo this; a warm room is fine. When the resin is fully hard, the surface can be rubbed down with progressively finer grades of wet and dry paper. It is important to always use this wet, with soapy water, as if sanded dry very unpleasant and potentially dangerous dust will be produced – once again, even when sanding wet, use a face mask. It is very likely that the weave of the glasscloth will show through a single coat of resin, especially if you have scraped off as much as you should. This standard of finish is fine for practical purposes; if you desire a glassy showroom finish, and can afford the weight, time and energy, then apply a further *thin* coat of resin and, when fully cured, attack it with the wet and dry finishing off with a liquid abrasive such as *Brasso* and then polish the surface. For this kind of finish to be effective, the standard of construction underneath needs to be beyond reproach – a full gloss finish just turns a badly built model into a shiny badly built model!

The epoxy glass finish is naturally excellent for scale models of full-size glassfibre sailplanes, but it is also almost mandatory for heavyweight slope cross-country and speed (F3F) models, slope pylon racers, multi-task (F3B) models and the more sophisticated thermal soarers.

From the high technology glass finish, back now to the basic modelling covering of tissue, nylon or silk. Actually, silk is not much used now; nylon can be recommended for general purpose slope soaring models with open structure wings, or for use on sheet balsa fuselages of any kind where it will add enormous strength and produce a very durable finish. The great advantage of a tissue and dope or nylon and dope finish is that it does produce a stressed skin effect which adds greatly to the torsional stiffness of components – particularly important where wings and tail planes are concerned. The disadvantage with tissue is that it is easily punctured, but of late a compromise has appeared that combines some of the best features of film and tissue covering which makes it eminently suitable for open structure models of small to medium (100 inch) size. This involves first covering the open areas of the airframe with thin (5 or 10 micron thick) mylar, applied like the non-adhesive backed films.

The idea is to combine the undoubted structural rigidity of a tissue finish with a higher level of puncture resistance. Film coverings are excellent and practical materials for many applications; it is just that, particularly when applied to a structure which relies on a tight skin for much of its torsional stiffness (as typically found, for instance, in lightweight soarers, electric sport models and most vintage types), films, and most of the fabrics, leave a lot to be desired.

It is not the intention to run film covering products down – at the very least they are un-

doubtedly an easy and quick route to a decent finish, and at best the results produced with them by the better builders are quite outstanding. It is also appreciated that not everyone finds the smell of dope as acceptable as does my wife – if there is not at least a faint whiff of cellulose about the house at all times she thinks I am sickening for something! The technique here described is neither as quick, easy or odour-free as film. But for an open-frame structure, the results produced are, without doubt, as good in terms of finish and puncture resistance and definitely superior when it comes to torsional rigidity.

You have to be prepared to work carefully with the mylar/tissue system. Preparation of the surface is as for a normal tissue/dope finish. Apply two or three coats of 40/60 dope/thinners, rubbing down gently with very worn sandpaper.

Rather more involved is the tissue over 5 micron Mylar finish on my **Sundancer 74** *prototype. Cellulose sprayed fuselage and ruling pen trim lines and lettering.*

One now has to apply adhesive around the edges of the open area and anywhere else that the mylar must adhere. *Evostick* contact adhesive, thinned to water consistency with *Evostick* cleaner (which is largely toluene, so be careful about ventilation) and applied with a fine brush works well, the heat-sensitive adhesives sold for use with film are equally good. A thin line all around the area, and along the top of each rib or spacer is all you need.

When the adhesive is completely dry to the touch, prepare the mylar. Frankly, this is a bit like Mrs Beeton's famous rabbit pie recipe which begins ".....first catch your rabbit"! The 5 micron mylar is *very* thin and quickly picks up static. Cutting it with scissors is a bit like milking a flea; the best method is to tape the stuff down and cut it with a new scalpel and steel ruler. It is actually worth going to the trouble of making a card template to cut around, especially if (as is often the case with wings) you need four identical pieces. The other way is to cut it on a marked out cutting mat, using the grid on the mat for reference to decide on the size. The mylar is fixed by tacking with a moderately hot iron. A lot of care is required to avoid ironing in creases on the adhesive lines. Once attached all round, the iron setting is wound right up and the mylar shrunk tight, the excess being trimmed off with the scalpel afterwards. The material is sufficiently thin so that the edges around the open areas will be inconspicuous once the tissue is applied. You will do very well to avoid some little wrinkles in the corner of some bays, but once again, these cease to be a problem once the tissue is on.

Some of the free-flight contest specialists use rather a different method, involving covering the whole of the surface, sheeted areas too, in mylar, This seems to work well for them, but there is no real need for it as the above described system is equally effective.

My favourite method for tissue covering is to cover with the tissue wet using thinners as the adhesive; brushed through the covering over the

Offset all-tissue colour scheme on my broad chord light-weight **Northern Light** *two metre model which also comes in an electric version. The fuselage is sprayed with car cellulose.*

sheeted areas this softens the dope on the airframe and quickly bonds. Using this technique, as the water dries out, a certain amount of white 'blush' marks will appear; do not worry, these will vanish with the first coat of dope. However, to minimise this blushing, always use the highest grade of cellulose thinners (three grades are normally available in five litre cans in auto accessory shops; the premium grade is the one to go for) and always work in reasonable temperatures, say 60 degrees or more. Once the tissue is dry, it is doped normally, using well thinned dope (normal model shop strength dope will need mixing 50/50 dope/thinners). It seems all wrong to be doping over a mylar film, but the tissue and mylar bond together beautifully. Light or medium grades of *Esaki Jap* tissue give excellent results producing a nice waterproof finish with a minimum of dope, but any *good* light-weight modelling tissue should be suitable.

Most experienced modellers have their own techniques for tissue or, come to that, nylon covering, but many present day modellers have never used these materials. While the method described, with the tissue wet, onto a pre-doped framework and using thinners to soften the dope

Beautiful scale fabric finish on Martin Simon's scale **Kirby Kite.**

and provide a bond gives excellent results, other modellers cover dry using paste and then water shrink, it is really a matter of personal choice. Both the mylar and the *Esaki* tissue are available from free-flight specialist suppliers.

The use of nylon as a covering medium is really restricted to larger models, or to those areas where extra strength is required – for example, the sheet balsa fuselage of a general purpose slope soaring model. Once again, the preferred technique is to cover with the nylon wet onto a pre-doped airframe, but this time, instead of brushing through with plain thinners, 50/50 dope/thinners is used to give a stronger bond. Once dry the nylon can be doped until airproof and waterproof. This does mean rather a lot of dope, and hence a nylon finish is not light. Some care is needed in selecting the grade of nylon to use – too thick will be both difficult to handle and also very heavy. It should also be remembered that, like the heat-shrink fabric coverings, nylon will easily warp a light airframe if carelessly applied and over-doped. The big advantage of nylon is its strength, and the way in which it will reinforce and hold together structures. As a clubmate of mine said; "...at least when you crash a nylon covered model you have a bag to take the bits home in!"

When it comes to applying colour to your model, remember that decoration is generally parasitic; it will not make the model fly any better, and if taken to extremes, adding extra weight, may well make it fly a good deal worse.

By careful forethought attractive and complex colour schemes can be executed both in film and tissue covering with little or no weight penalty, so that the use of paint, either brush or spray applied, can be limited to such areas as fibreglass fuselages. It is worthwhile thinking about how the model will look in its normal environment – a slope soarer with the top surface finished in a tasteful shade of green may look nice, but the first time the pilot is struggling to fly it in difficult conditions a couple of hundred feet below him above a bracken covered hillside, green will not seem such a good idea! Similarly, a white thermal soaring model can look very smart, but white models disappear with alarming rapidity at twelve or thirteen hundred feet in certain light conditions.

It is a good idea to provide a contrast in the finish of the model and experience shows that an underside finished in a dark strong colour – black, red, dark blue etc., coupled with a bright, light top surface, yellow, orange or white, with some decor in other colours – gives the best assistance in keeping the model in sight and judging its attitude. A patch of metallised mylar or foil on one wing leading edge can also be useful, catching the sun as the model circles and giving a clear indication of the direction in which it is going.

If one point is worth re-emphasising on covering and finishing it is that of surface preparation. Irrespective of the final finish to be applied, the better the basic surface the better the finished article will look. Do not be afraid of using sandpaper and do not ignore small holes and discontinuities – use an appropriate filler (a flexible one such as *Isopon P38* is excellent for small holes, while for bigger areas one of the specialist lightweight modelling fillers or a combination of microballoons and sanding sealer can be used). Do not neglect the important stage of dust removal from the model and area before starting to apply the finish. Time spent at the preparation stage will be repaid many times over by the quality of the final finish.

CHAPTER 11

Learning to fly – the basics

Whether the new modeller has elected to go the ready-to-fly route or to build his own model from a kit or plan, sooner or later, he will be confronted by the **first flight** – after all that is what he built/bought the thing for, isn't it?

The thing which needs to be said first, second, third and ad infinitum about this stage is ... GET HELP. Flying a radio controlled model aeroplane is at least as difficult as learning to drive a car, in fact in my opinion it is good deal more difficult. If the newcomer tries to go it alone, he will undoubtedly crash his model. Sad as this is, it pales into insignificance alongside the prospect of the errant model striking some person or piece of property and causing damage to it. At which point it is worthwhile stating what may seem like too obvious – get third party public liability insurance to cover your model flying activities. Even a relatively small R/C sailplane could cause serious injury or, in extreme circumstances, death if it were to come into collision with a human being. Horrendous as the contemplation of such an event may seem, it would be foolhardy to not have insurance to mitigate the financial penalties involved in it, or in some lesser incident.

The best way to obtain reliable insurance cover for model flying is to join the British Model Flying Association, either as an individual or preferably through one of their many affiliated clubs. It is possible to arrange individual insurance, but the drawbacks and pitfalls of this are many, and it is unlikely to be less expensive. Referring back to the above statement about the need to get help with the initial stages of learning to fly, joining a club will, of course, immediately put the newcomer in touch with experienced modellers who can help him through the early stages of adjusting his first glider and learning to fly it.

Ensuring that a model will fly successfully starts out, not at the flying field or slope, but in the workshop. There are a number of essential checks which will go a long way towards guaranteeing success.

The longitudinal balance point of the model – usually referred to as the CG (centre of gravity) *must* be in the place specified on the plan. Depending upon the model type and the wing planform, this will be anywhere from 25 to 40 per cent of the root wing chord back from the leading edge. It will normally be necessary to add ballast to the nose of a glider to achieve the required balance point; it may seem a shame to add weight to your carefully constructed model, but it has to be done.

The model should balance laterally when fully assembled ready for flight i.e., one wing should not be heavier than the other. While not as crucial as correct location of the longitudinal balance point, in that small deviations will not prevent the model from flying altogether, it is worthwhile taking the trouble to get this right.

The flying surfaces should be firmly attached to the fuselage by whatever is the design method – rubber bands, bolts or plug-together using wire dowels – and they must be properly aligned so that the wing and tail are both at 90 degrees to the fuselage centre line in plan view, and when viewed from the front there is no tilt of the flying surfaces.

The tail fin must be vertical and properly aligned with the fuselage centre-line in plan view.

The angles at which the wing and tail are set in relation to the fuselage datum line in side view (the angle of incidence) must be as shown on the plan.

When viewed from the front there must be no twists in the wing or tail surfaces. The exception here is if some deliberate washout – trailing edge up in relation to leading edge – has been built into the wings in accordance with the plan, a feature sometimes found on beginners' models as it is an aid to stability by preventing tip stalling in flight. If washout is built in, it must be equal on both sides. Twists in flying surfaces are known as warps, and a badly warped wing or tailplane can make a model virtually impossible to fly. Any warp should be removed by gently applying heat with a heatgun or fan heater while twisting the surfaces in the opposite direction, and then holding them in this position as they cool. (Note: if warps have been built into a foam cored/veneer wing, or a fully sheeted one, it may be almost impossible to remove them.) Do not forget to also check the vertical fin/rudder to make sure that there are no warps in this.

The control surfaces (which will normally be limited to rudder and elevator on a beginner's slope or thermal soarer) should be in line with the fin or tailplane when the transmitter trim controls for these functions are set in neutral i.e. in the centre of their travel. In the case of the all-moving tailplane as commonly fitted to many thermal-soaring models, where there is no fixed surface with which to align the control surface, then ensure, by measurement, that the neutral position is as indicated on the plan.

The movements of the control surfaces in response to movements of the transmitter control sticks must be smooth and free from any jamming or sticking throughout the full range. The total movement at full stick deflection should be as specified on the plan (if lacking this information, then a movement, measured at the trailing edge of the surface, of ¾" each way for rudder and ¼" each way for elevator is a reasonable place to start). If the transmitter is fitted with rate switches which cut down the movement of the main controls when switched in, adjust these to give approximately 60 per cent of the movement recommended. Needless to say, when the rudder control stick is moved to the left, the rudder (as viewed from the rear) should move to the left and vice-versa. When the elevator stick is moved forward i.e. towards the top of the transmitter, the elevator must move to down and vice-versa.

All the above may sound like a lot of checking, but applying it to all new models – not just the first one – can save a lot of problems later on in the test flying.

Finally, then, before departing to the slope or flying field, in company with your instructor, make sure that the batteries in the transmitter and the receiver power pack are fully charged, and make sure that both the transmitter and receiver are switched off before packing the model in the car.

Traditionally, the first stages in test flying a model aircraft involve hand-launched glides, during which the model can be adjusted to glide smoothly – neither diving too steeply or rearing up and then dropping in a stall – and it can be

A good demonstration of the correct launching technique for test gliding a new model – in this case an electric soarer.

established that no unexpected turning tendencies are present. Frankly, if the model is set up straight and true, and the checks listed above have been carefully carried out, hand gliding can provide very little information for a radio controlled glider, and many experienced modellers will dispense with it altogether. Certainly, since the model is close to the ground, if there is any wind or turbulence about (as there almost inevitably will be close to a slope-soaring site), hand gliding can be quite dangerous as a sudden gust can turn the model onto a wing tip with damaging results.

In general, be guided by your instructor in the matter of hand gliding; if he prefers to either launch the model straight out into the lift from the slope, or in the case of a thermal soarer put it straight on the towline, then fine.

The weather conditions for the first flight of a new model, and for the first attempts at controlling it by a new modeller, should be as near to the optimum as possible. For slope soaring this will

mean a steady wind of between 5 and 10 knots blowing squarely onto a known slope i.e. a slope which is known to produce good smooth lift. For a thermal model, a gentle breeze of 3 or 4 knots blowing from a consistent direction over a flat, unobstructed field is ideal. Flat calm, while obviously useless for the slope soarer, in that no lift will be generated, is also not really desirable for the thermal model as a little breeze will ensure a good launch. Stronger winds can be handled once the model is known to be properly adjusted and the pilot has gained some level of competence, but stronger winds mean turbulence and should be avoided in the learning stages.

Assuming that the model has been launched, flown and found to be satisfactory by an experienced pilot, what should the newcomer do on first trying his hand with the transmitter? Since the techniques required for flying slope and thermal models differ somewhat from this point onwards, it would be best to consider them separately.

Learning to fly a slope soarer

The first point to appreciate is that, as the pilot will be standing on the edge of the slope, facing the wind, the model must always be kept in front of him. This is, to some extent, an advantage, as the amount of time which the model will spend flying towards the pilot will be limited, and it is this flight attitude which poses the biggest problem for the trainee R/C pilot. Why? Well, unlike the full-size situation where, with the pilot sitting in the aircraft, left is always left and right always right, the model pilot suffers a type of visual control reversal when the model is flying towards him – if the model is turning to its left, it will be moving to the pilot's **right**, and this confuses the situation since **right** stick is needed to correct the turn – see Figure 11.1.

Eventually, reaction to this becomes automatic, and the appropriate directional control

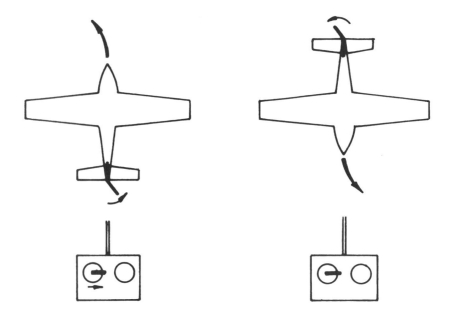

(A) MODEL FLYING AWAY AND TURNING LEFT. RIGHT CONTROL CORRECTION IS NATURAL

(B) MODEL FLYING TOWARDS OPERATOR AND TURNING LEFT. RIGHT CONTROL CORRECTION IS UNNATURAL

Figure 11.1 *Visual control reversal problem.*

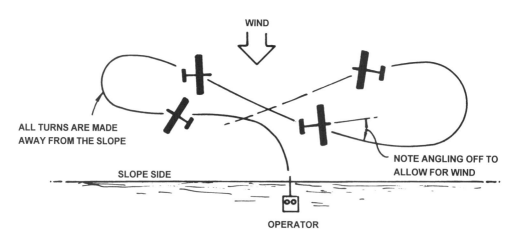

WIND

ALL TURNS ARE MADE AWAY FROM THE SLOPE

NOTE ANGLING OFF TO ALLOW FOR WIND

SLOPE SIDE

OPERATOR

Figure 11.2 *First slope flights.*

will be applied without thinking, but in the early stages of learning to fly it can be a major problem. There are a couple of tips which help, and these work with either rudder or aileron. To correct a turn when the model is flying towards the pilot, either put the stick under the low wing, or, repeat silently "if it's going right, give it right". The thing *not* to do is to twist around to try and get into the same orientation as the model, finishing up by flying it while looking over one shoulder – this is a bad habit to get into, and one which is hard to shake off once acquired.

The principal aim during first slope flights should be to keep the model a sensible distance away from the slope face, in the area of good lift and avoid, at all costs, turning downwind. The

Total concentration on the model is necessary in the early stages of learning to fly.

illustration in Fig. 11.2 shows how to do this – angle the model to left or right, keeping the nose pointing 30 degrees or so out from the slope and let it fly along the slope. The wind will gradually push it back towards the slope, and once it has flown off fifty or sixty yards to one side, a turn **away** from the slope can be made and the model allowed to fly back across the front of the pilot and off in the opposite direction, once again angling it into wind. In this way a sort of figure eight pattern is flown and the model is never turned completely downwind towards the slope. Why not turn downwind? Well, in even a fairly gentle breeze, a downwind turn will be elongated in relation to the ground, and by the time the model is once again facing into wind and out from the slope, it will most likely be back over the brow of the slope, vertically over the pilot, or worse still behind him. This is *not* a desirable position for a model being flown by a novice!

Landing a slope soarer is something that cannot be learned from a book! Every slope will have a different pattern of airflow and different lift and sink areas. The main aim is to land the model into wind, at the point of maximum airflow over the slope, as this will give the slowest ground speed. Later, in advanced slope flying, the technique of doing this by using the slope lift will be described, but in the early stages, the beginner should stick to slopes which have a long flat area behind them, so that the model may be allowed to drift back and then landed straight towards the slope in this level area, where the airflow will be fairly constant and predictable.

Even very experienced slope R/C pilots sometimes get into trouble when landing in difficult conditions, so the occasional cartwheel or wing tip landing is nothing to be ashamed of. Frankly, during the early stages of learning slope soaring, most landings will be of this type, hence the need for the slope training model to be a rugged and forgiving design, with features such as rubber band attached wings, which will absorb a reasonable amount of abuse.

This electric soarer demonstrates the correct, shallow climb angle for these low powered models.

As with all R/C flying, a problem will be encountered in the early days of learning to fly with the co-ordination of the rudder and elevator functions throughout the flight. Assuming that the model is properly adjusted to fly straight and level in calm conditions, hands off, when rudder is applied the nose will inevitably drop, the flying speed will increase and, when the rudder is neutralised and the turn cancelled with a little opposite rudder, the excess speed will cause the nose to rise and the model will stall. If a full 360-degree turn is attempted, the nose will drop so much that the model will enter a spiral dive. To avoid these problems, elevator input is required – a little up to hold the nose up during the turn, some down to avoid the zoom and stall effect as the turn is cancelled. It is this co-ordinating of the two controls which poses a problem for the beginner. The best way to approach the co-ordination problem in the early stages is to avoid it. To make a turn, apply a little rudder, and as soon as the nose starts to drop ease off the rudder, apply a little elevator to resume level flight and after returning the elevator to neutral, repeat the process until the desired degree of turn has been accomplished. Naturally, this will make the flying a little jerky, but, surprisingly quickly the separate rudder and elevator operations will start to blend together naturally to produce co-ordinated turns.

Learning to fly on the slope is at once more and less difficult than learning to fly a thermal model on a flat field. More difficult because the necessary wind blowing over the undulating terrain will produce air movements which will upset the model and need corrective action that the beginner will, at first, find difficult to apply quickly and accurately. Less difficult because the continuous lift which the slope will produce will sustain the model and enable long flying sessions to be undertaken, with the instructor taking the transmitter back as required to sort out the inevitable problems, then returning it to the trainee for more practice.

Learning to fly a thermal soarer

Thermal models are launched using a towline, either a simple line with the necessary power input provided by a person running, or a composite line of nylon monofilament with a proportion (usually 20%) of rubber which, when stretched, will provide the necessary energy to tow up the model. In operation, a ring slips over a towhook which is located just in front of the CG of the model, and the model is launched into wind and rises like a kite. If properly adjusted, no control inputs should really be necessary on the tow launch, other than a little rudder to counter any swing off-line caused by side gusts. See Figure 11.3.

For early flights, the tow launch should always be undertaken by the instructor, and the transmitter passed to the trainee only once the

(A) BUNGEE SET UP, UNSTRETCHED

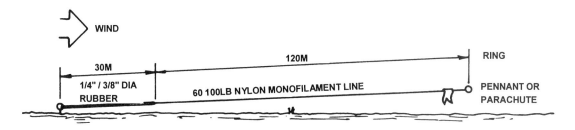

WIND

30M

120M

RING

1/4" / 3/8" DIA RUBBER

60 100LB NYLON MONOFILAMENT LINE

PENNANT OR PARACHUTE

(B) READY TO LAUNCH

WIND

TYPICALLY STRETCHED TO 100M

(C) POINT OF RELEASE FROM LINE

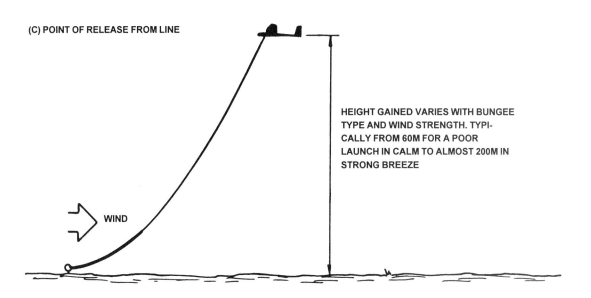

HEIGHT GAINED VARIES WITH BUNGEE TYPE AND WIND STRENGTH. TYPICALLY FROM 60M FOR A POOR LAUNCH IN CALM TO ALMOST 200M IN STRONG BREEZE

WIND

Figure 11.3 *Bungee launching a thermal soarer.*

A top thermal competitor and his timekeeper concentrating on eking out that last few seconds of lift.

model has flown clear of the line and settled back to its normal gliding speed and angle.

The actual flying, provided that strong wind conditions are avoided, should be easier than on the slope. Naturally, since the pilot will not be able to recognise or use thermal lift at this stage, each flight will simply be a downward glide from the tow launch (normally from a 150 metre long line). Once again, the advice of using controls one at a time initially applies, but as the airflow over the flat site should be smoother than that over a slope, the model should suffer less disturbance, and, if properly adjusted, it should almost be possible to fly it from launch to landing without using the elevator control, simply steering it around the sky with the rudder. Although the restriction on making downwind turns which is necessary in early flights on the slope does not apply on the flat field, it is sensi-

Good launch technique for this 100S class model on the towline – nose up and lots of line tension to ensure a clean, rapid getaway.

ble to keep the model upwind of the pilot until making the actual landing circuit. There are two secrets to getting the model round and pointing into wind for the landing without problems; first, make the whole of the landing circuit in front of the pilot, thus minimising the visually reversed control problems. Secondly, do not attempt to make a full 360 degree circuit in one go, but turn no more than 90 degrees at a time, with straight legs in between to settle the model down – see Figure 11.4.

Once the final into wind turn has been made, even if the model is higher than you would like do not be tempted to try another turn, as this will more often than not be fatal! Keep it straight and land straight ahead, easing in just a little up elevator when the model is almost down. Better a

walk of 90 or 100 metres to pick up the model than a pile of wreckage.

As confidence and skill increase the landing circuit can be pushed back until the final leg is being flown towards the pilot, and at this stage landing accuracy will begin to improve until the pilot is capable of spot landings. However, it is still good practice to make a square circuit with distinct 90-degree turns and straight legs in between, adjusting the length of the legs to suit the wind strength so that the final landing takes place in the desired location.

With a thermal soarer, the launch and landing will be the things which are mastered last, as the normal flying around the sky of these generally stable and gentle models will be relatively easy to learn, at least in light wind conditions. However,

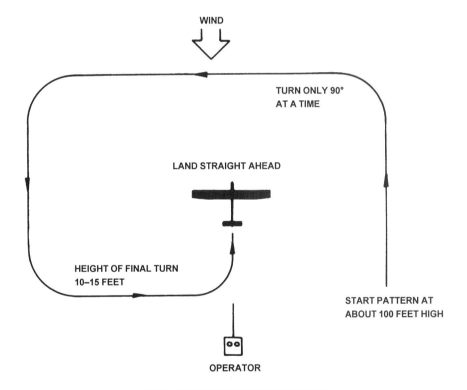

Figure 11.4 *First landing circuits on the flat field.*

since every flight must contain a launch and a landing, until the learner is confident in these phases he should not fly unless an experienced pilot is on hand to sort out any problems.

Summary

Once the beginner can launch his model from slope or line, fly it around the sky in reasonable conditions and land it within 20 or 30 yards without damage, he will be ready to start to learn the skills of lift detection and use which make sailplane flying so different from flying powered radio controlled models, and the subsequent chapters concentrate on these aspects. However, it is emphasised that, in order to use lift, complete and confident control of the model in all attitudes and situations is needed. Although the basic business of getting the model up and down safely in one piece may be mastered in the space of a few weeks of intensive practice, many more hours will be necessary to attain the automatic reflexes of the experienced slope or thermal pilot that facilitate proper exploitation of the lift.

CHAPTER 12

Advanced slope flying

Once the new slope pilot has reached the stage where he can comfortably control his model in all situations, and land it most times without problems, he will probably find that simply going up to his favourite slope in decent conditions and flying no longer provides sufficient buzz. There are several ways forward from here:

- Explore other slopes and conditions which provide more marginal lift. This can be done using the same model with which the pilot learned to fly i.e. a typical slope trainer, but it will be more fun – and a good deal easier – with a cleaner, faster flying model, possibly one with ailerons. A good 100 inch thermal soarer will also be useful for those really light wind days. It is amazing how many flyable slopes can be found in an area, some of them most unpromising at first sight. Do take care that you are not flying just around the corner from another group of modellers, though, and do be careful to seek permission on slopes that have an obvious private owner.
- Expand into scale models – either pukka sailplanes or PSS. There is enough variation here to keep the modeller satisfied for several lifetimes!

- Specialise in one of the contest classes – either the speed classes, pylon racing or F3F, the aerobatic class (which, sadly, does not seem to be flown much at major contests these days) or cross country. The skills needed in each of these classes are different, as are the model types.

Whichever one of the above options interests the modeller, there are certain advanced slope flying skills which he will need to acquire. One of the most important of these is the slope-side landing. Proficiency in this manoeuvre opens up all sorts of slopes which have no easy or obvious landing area available. The essence of the manoeuvre is to place the model in a skidding turn just in the area of maximum wind velocity a few feet above the slope edge, so that it can be 'plopped' down next to the pilot with virtually no ground speed. Once mastered it is a very safe way of landing, due to the low ground speed. However, if misjudged it can result in the model flying into the hill while travelling at full speed downwind. In such a confrontation between a few pounds of wood and glassfibre and countless millions of tons of mountain, there is only one winner!

Fortunately, the slope-side (or slope-edge) landing can be approached by degrees. The way to start is to dive the model down the face of the slope, trying to stay a fixed distance above the ground i.e. descending at the same rate as the hill. This dive should be placed 20 or 30 yards out to one side of the pilot's position. The model is then turned through 90 degrees towards the pilot and flown across the face of the slope and then, when 10 or 15 yards past the pilot's position (and this is the tricky part), turned towards the slope and flown up the face. The extra speed acquired in the dive out and the lift coming up the face of the slope should ensure that it stays clear of the ground. Just as the model approaches the top of the slope, a flat, skidding 180-degree turn towards the pilot is started. Ideally the model should breast the crest of the hill just as it completes this turn, coming into wind just above the ridge in the area of maximum wind strength. This coupled with the speed lost during the turn should bring the model almost to a standstill in terms of ground speed, while the rapid airflow over the surfaces should still ensure full control authority.

Start practising the manoeuvre too high, so that the model skids out of its final turn 15 or 20 feet up. It can be held briefly in the hover at this point and then, by applying down elevator, pushed out into the lift again. Keep repeating the approach at the same speed and in the same groove, but a little lower each time, until the final turn is skidding into wind only 4 or 5 feet above the top of the ridge. You will find that the wind speed is quite a lot higher at this height than it was at 20 feet, and it will be correspondingly easier to hold the hover. Once you can do this consistently, it is simply a matter of applying an extra dab of down as the ground speed drops to zero and the model will simply sink to the ground vertically. If the model has air brakes or flaps, they can be deployed just before applying the final dab of down.

This procedure sounds somewhat horrifying

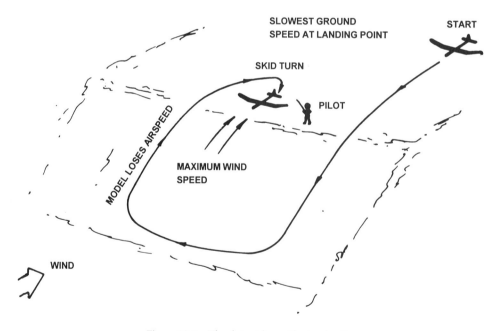

Figure 12.1 *The slope side or ridge top landing.*

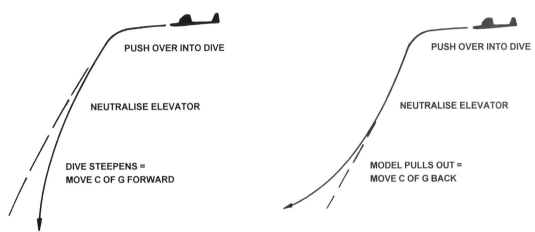

(A) C OF G TOO FAR BACK

PUSH OVER INTO DIVE

NEUTRALISE ELEVATOR

DIVE STEEPENS =
MOVE C OF G FORWARD

(B) C OF G TOO FAR FORWARD

PUSH OVER INTO DIVE

NEUTRALISE ELEVATOR

MODEL PULLS OUT =
MOVE C OF G BACK

Figure 12.2 *Adjusting an aerobatic slope soarer.*

when written down in cold blood, but since it can be approached by degrees, in practice it is quite easy to learn. Needless to say there are some slopes – near vertical cliffs for example – which are not suitable for this technique, and other methods of placing the model just above the ground in the desired landing area have to be devised. The main thing is to identify the area of maximum airflow over the slope and use this information to minimise the model's ground speed on touchdown.

To state the obvious, if the aim is to fly aerobatics, then an aerobatic model will be required. The typical rudder elevator slope trainer will perform very decent loops, some sort of barrel roll, a stall turn and, if the lift is really good, it may be persuaded to stay inverted for a little while. Once the modeller progresses beyond this 'schedule', then a proper aerobatic slope soarer will be required. Such a model will have powerful ailerons, a bi-convex semi-symmetrical or fully symmetrical wing to permit full inverted performance and, unlike the trainer, it will have little natural or self stability and will require constant attention from the pilot – it will have to be

flown all the time. Obviously before acquiring such a model, the pilot should be thoroughly proficient with his original trainer. It may also be worthwhile to take an intermediate step such as building a second wing for the trainer with ailerons and reduced dihedral in order to become used to the rather different technique involved in flying an aileron model.

When it comes to adjusting an aerobatic slope soarer for flight, then there is a simple trick which will be a great help in achieving the desired neutral stability. Place the model off to one side and push it into a dive of about 30 degrees, then release the elevator control to neutral and watch the model. It will either gradually pull out of the dive, gradually dive more steeply, or simply continue at the same angle until pulled out by the application of up elevator. If the latter is the case – congratulations, the model is just right! If it tends to dive more steeply, then add just a little ballast to the nose, move the CG forward a little, and try again. If it tends to pull out itself, remove a little nose ballast, move the CG back, and try again. This may sound wrong, but be assured it is correct. By proceeding a little at a time, the desired

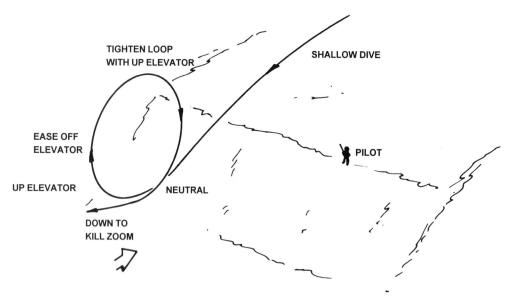

**TIGHTEN LOOP
WITH UP ELEVATOR**

SHALLOW DIVE

**EASE OFF
ELEVATOR**

PILOT

UP ELEVATOR

NEUTRAL

**DOWN TO
KILL ZOOM**

Figure 12.3   *First loops.*

state where the model continues to point in the direction commanded until pulled out by an application of opposite control will be achieved. Needless to say, the model should fly completely straight with the controls in neutral, so a true, straight, airframe is required, as correcting any natural turn by applying permanent aileron offset will cause great problems at different air speeds.

The easiest aerobatic figure to understand, and to perform, is the loop. To start with, fly these directly into wind, out from the slope face. Dive the model to acquire extra speed (a longer, shallow dive is much better than a short steep one), then pull in up elevator. If the elevator is just banged to full, then the model probably will loop, but the resultant manoeuvre will be clumsy, with the model flopping over the top as the drag of the large elevator movement and sudden change of pitch angle rapidly bleeds off the air speed. The aim is to use sufficient elevator to fly the model around the loop without losing too much air speed. The effect of the wind will be to blow the model back towards the slope, elongating the loop and spoiling its shape. If sufficient air speed

is maintained throughout, the elevator can be used to vary the radius of the loop to correct this tendency. In order to judge the shape of the loop, it must be flown off to one side of the pilot's position, rather than directly in front of him.

Once a single loop can be flown accurately, a second, consecutive one can follow superimposed on the first. Speed is all important here, sufficient being required to provide good control response forcing the model to follow eactly the same track as constant as possible throughout the two loops – easier said than done! When three consecutive loops can be flown with reasonable accuracy, there is little point in going further. The trick then is to be able to do the same thing parallel to the slope – across wind! This is *not* easy, as the model will be blown sideways, and corrective aileron and sometimes rudder too will need to be fed in during the loops, which in itself can cause the pattern to 'screw' out of true. The only trick is to keep practising until the necessary corrective tweaks of control become automatic.

The outside loop, or bunt as it is sometimes called, is simply the reverse of the loop – a com-

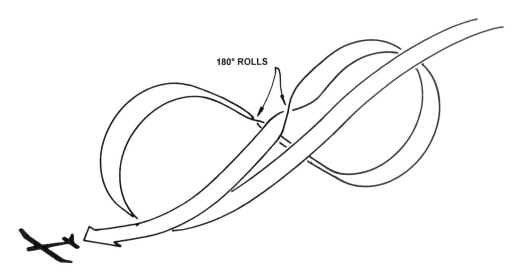

180° ROLLS

Figure 12.4 *Cuban Eight.*

plete 360-degree circle in a vertical plane but in a **downward** direction. This is best mastered after the pilot has learned to fly inverted.

Inverted flight, with a proper aerobatic model, is a fairly simple matter. All that is required is to remember that the elevator is reversed – up to dive down to climb. In this respect, it helps if the model *looks* different when inverted, an appropriate colour scheme can help here. The directional controls, aileron and, surprisingly, rudder are *not* reversed. Inverted should be practised until the model can confidently be flown around for several minutes like this, including 360-degree turns in both directions.

Once inverted has been conquered, the outside loop can be approached in exactly the same way as the inside one, but flown from the inverted position. Only when absolutely confident of the model's turning radius on down elevator should outside loops be started the proper way – from upright **downwards**.

Figure eights are simply a matter of combining an inside and outside loop in either a horizontal or, much more difficult, vertical plane.

There is one exception to this, the Cuban Eight, which consists of two inside loops with a half roll in the middle.

Rolling manoeuvres are started with some excess speed generated by a shallow dive, and again should be practised initially into wind, away from the slope. Any good aerobatic model will roll rapidly on full aileron, if travelling at a decent speed, and corrective rudder and elevator to maintain a straight course will hardly be required during a single roll. If two or more are to be performed consecutively, it will be necessary to start introducing little dabs of elevator (up when upright, down when inverted) and rudder (top rudder when the model is on its side) to prevent the rolls from wandering off course, and the correct application of these adjustments is the key to performing good consecutive rolls. The slower the roll, the more precise and important become the corrections. The slow roll is thus much the most difficult figure to perform, and is best approached via a hesitation roll, where, by releasing the aileron control and then re-applying it, the model is made to dwell for a second in

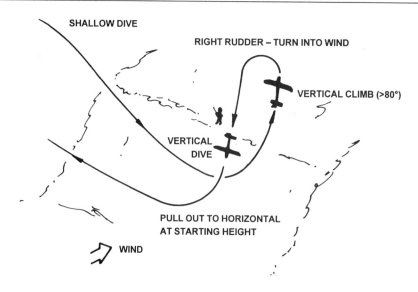

SHALLOW DIVE

RIGHT RUDDER – TURN INTO WIND

VERTICAL CLIMB (>80°)

VERTICAL DIVE

PULL OUT TO HORIZONTAL AT STARTING HEIGHT

WIND

Figure 12.5 *Stall turn.*

each of the 90-degree stations – upright, 90-degree left bank, inverted, 90-degree right bank. Finite rudder and elevator corrections will be needed at each station, and after perfecting this, the integration of these corrections in the continuous slow roll will be easier to master. Once again, when proficient, rolls should be presented across the slope.

Most other figures are combinations of full and half loops and outside loops with full and half rolls – the previously mentioned Cuban Eight for example. Two of these, the reversal (half roll followed by half loop) and Immelman (half loop followed by half roll) are the standard and convenient method of turning an aerobatic model through 180 degrees. Two exceptions which need examining separately are the stall turn and spin.

Properly performed the stall turn is a graceful and satisfying figure – get it wrong and the result is a mess with the model tumbling about with zero air speed. This is one aerobatic manoeuvre which should be practised across wind (parallel to the slope) from the start, as crosswind is a positive aid to performing it. From the usual

shallow entry dive, after a brief level flight passage, pull the model into a climb, gradually steepening to 80 degrees as speed bleeds off. Before speed is completely lost give the model a little jab of rudder *away* from the slope, neutralise, and with luck the model will rotate in a flat turn reversing direction until it is diving to gain speed, then pull out at the same height as the entry. The key is in turning *away* from the slope so that the wind is helping to flick the back end of the model round. The wings need to be kept level with aileron throughout, and a lot of practice is required to get it right – ideally the model should turn just as it stops climbing, if it is still moving and under command then technically the figure is a wing over rather than a stall turn.

The spin needs to be entered from a good height. Not all models will spin easily, and, it should be said, that there is the odd one which once in a proper flat spin refuses to recover! With the model at a good height, well out from the slope, start to ease the nose up until it is just on the point of stalling and bang in full rudder in the desired direction of the spin and full up el-

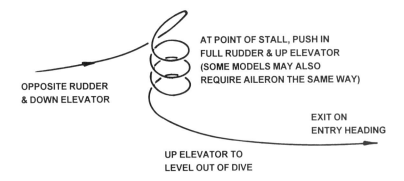

AT POINT OF STALL, PUSH IN
FULL RUDDER & UP ELEVATOR
(SOME MODELS MAY ALSO
REQUIRE AILERON THE SAME WAY)

OPPOSITE RUDDER
& DOWN ELEVATOR

EXIT ON
ENTRY HEADING

UP ELEVATOR TO
LEVEL OUT OF DIVE

Figure 12.6   *Three turn spin.*

evator. If the model refuses to spin, try again, but this time add full aileron in the same direction. If the result is still a spiral dive rather than a fully developed, stalled, spin then either more up elevator, possibly more rudder or a more rearward CG (which may not be possible as it will upset

*Gordon Rae shows his **Skew Ball** 60 inch slope pylon racer design with novel asymmetric tail layout to veteran radio enthusiast Bill Trow. Bill was flying radio control gliders as far back as 1950!*

the normal trim of the model) will be necessary to get this particular model to enter a spin.

Leaving a spin is normally simply a matter of neutralising the controls about half a turn away from the desired exit heading. If the model does not stop spinning, opposite rudder and down elevator will normally do the trick. The inverted spin is exactly the same, except that down elevator is used to enter it (from inverted, of course) and up elevator to exit in an inverted dive.

It is fairly easy for the sport aerobatic slope pilot to learn to throw his model around the sky in quite spectacular fashion; what must be remembered though is that, without a power unit and relying upon trading height for speed to carry out the aerobatics, care must be taken to keep the model flying smoothly all the time, conserving energy gained on the exit from one figure for entry into the next and utilising the areas of strongest slope lift to provide the extra speed needed for complex manoeuvres. Performing aerobatics to the precise standard required by competition judges is a great deal more difficult than carrying out a free-style aerobatic 'beat up', and the only way to achieve the required standard is to practise hard in all sorts of wind and lift conditions.

Even if aerobatic flying is not the eventual aim of the slope pilot, he would be well advised to master the basic rolling and looping manoeuvres,

Proof that the strange tail layout works – the **Skew Ball** *in flight over the Malverns.*

plus the spin and stall turn. In this way, whatever unusual attitude his model enters, he will not be at a loss. This applies particularly to the racing enthusiast, who intends to fly F3F (one at a time speed) or pylon race (two to four models at once racing against each other) as, in the heat of competition, it is very easy to put the model into odd positions.

Apart from total control of the model in all situations, the slope soarer who wishes to compete in the speed classes needs to cultivate a feel for the lift distribution found on various slopes in various conditions. This is because one of the keys to flying as fast as possible is to fly in the strongest area of lift. Quick reactions and good judgement to anticipate turns and (in multi-aircraft racing) avoid mid-air collisions are also pre-requisites, but, as with lift awareness these are all skills that can be practised and honed during sport flying sessions with club mates. One other skill that the racing pilot needs to develop is in the area of assessing when his particular model's speed could be improved by the addition of ballast to increase the wing loading. Again, this kind of data can only be obtained by flying the model in an extensive range of conditions on various

slopes and checking its performance against the stopwatch in different ballast states.

Even if there is no intention to fly in racing contests, a fast pylon race type model, of either the restricted 60 inch span class or the bigger and more sophisticated F3F type, makes a fine sport aerobatic and general slope soarer, particularly for stronger wind conditions, and many more of them are built for this purpose than for competitive racing.

Another model which is useful as a general purpose slope soarer is one specifically intended for cross-country contests. Here, since the model must be flown around a course, performing tasks en route which demand the shedding of height, and sometimes mean going a long way away from the slope lift areas, the emphasis is on good glide angle, good penetration and general excellent soaring performance. All of which make the better cross-country models excellent sport soarers in conditions ranging from calm, where thermal lift is needed to fly at all, up to quite strong winds.

In order to fly a cross-country slope model successfully, less knowledge of aerobatics is necessary than is the case with other classes, but to get the best out of them a real nose for the best lift areas has to be developed. The slope cross-country pilot will spend a lot of his time flying the model at extreme heights and distances, and will benefit from reading the next chapter concerning thermal soaring, as much of his flying will be in thermal lift, even though the flight starts out from the slope. It is not difficult to fly the average slope cross-country model; but it is a different matter to be able to squeeze the last little bit of performance out of it in marginal lift conditions. Once again the key is lots and lots of sport and practice flying with the model in all conditions, ranging far and wide from the initial slope launch and making use of every little bit of lift which presents itself.

CHAPTER 13

Advanced thermal flying

Once the thermal pilot can launch his model to the top of the towline consistently, and fly it smoothly around the sky to a safe landing close by, he is ready to turn his attention to finding and exploiting the thermal lift described in Chapter 4. More than any other branch of R/C soaring, thermal soaring is something which can only be truly learned hands on; the modeller who only flies a tow-launched glider occasionally will struggle to find lift on days when his well-practised clubmate is getting away almost every flight. An illustration of this occurred when I went to visit a club flying field one afternoon to demonstrate thermal soaring to a group of power R/C pilots who occasionally dabbled in gliders. I was promptly informed that there was "no lift on this field, the longest flight ever done with a glider is only 10 minutes." Eyeing a sky bubbling with fair weather cumulus, I was moved to offer drinks all round if I failed to do a flight in excess of 30 minutes from one of the first two launches, providing that the club would buy the beer if I did. This offer was eagerly accepted, and the first launch duly went away in a massive thermal for a flight well in excess of 90 minutes to win the beer and prove the point – practice is the key.

There are two main aspects to thermal flying – **detection** and **exploitation**.

Detecting lift

The first rule must be; look in the most likely place! This may seem a somewhat fatuous statement, but the fact is that all flying fields and their surroundings have some areas which are more favourable for thermal generation than others. Good areas are large stretches of tarmac or concrete (tennis courts, carparks etc.), large flat-roofed buildings, ploughed or stubble fields. Poor areas are woods (with one exception mentioned later), water, fields of long standing crops and plain grass areas.

However, the above breakdown of areas is only half the story; there are ground features which can turn an otherwise poor area into a prime lift generator. One of the commonest forms of thermal is the *wind shadow* thermal. If an area of otherwise unpromising ground is sheltered from the wind in the lee of a large building, small hill or other ground feature while being exposed to the full rays of the sun, it will heat up faster than the surrounding area which is being

Former World Champion Nic Wright prepares to fly his sleek aileron-equipped Electra *open class model.*

cooled by the wind. Such an area can become a regular source of bubbles of lift; on good days the frequency with which they break away and rise is so regular that it is extremely easy to predict when the next thermal will be along, based on the time gap between the last two.

Smaller ground features can also play a part in lift generation; a crosswind hedge will often trip lift on its downwind side, while small dips and hollows will cause variations in the heating pattern of the ground and, as was emphasised in Chapter 4, variations in temperature are the root cause of thermal generation.

The time of day can also play an important part in determining where lift will occur. Woodland, previously rated a poor thermal generator, comes into its own later in the day, an hour or so before sunset, when the general air temperature cools and the air among the trees thus becomes relatively warmer. There is often a gentle but sustained period of lift given off by woodland in the evening, and a similar effect can be found over small valleys.

What other clues are there for us to find in seeking lift? Perhaps the most obvious is the behaviour of other flying objects – other models and birds. It does not take long for an experienced thermal pilot to determine that the group

of seagulls circling stiff-winged across the field are exploiting a thermal, but the behaviour of smaller birds also needs to be watched carefully. In particular insect feeders such as swallows and swifts are a very useful marker of just-developing low-level lift. These birds are not soaring, but feeding, and a concentration of them in one area thus indicates a concentration of food – in this case insects which are being sucked up into the air by something – and that something is, more often than not, rising warm air, an embryo thermal.

Other birds, such as crows, rooks, kestrels etc. also soar on rising air, and the skylark also takes advantage of lift to carry out his vertical ascents until disappearing straight upwards.

Another glider in lift is also an infallible indicator – do not be ashamed of using someone else's thermal, but do have the good manners to circle in the same direction as any models already using the lift, or expect some candid remarks from the pilots!

Cumulus clouds, while they do mark the top of thermal columns, are really on too big a scale to be useful to the R/C thermal soarer – it is virtually impossible to judge whether one is really under the cloud or not. In any case, the thermal which is topped by the cloud will be leaning with the wind direction, so lift might only be present directly under the cloud immediately below cloudbase.

There is, however, one almost guaranteed thermal indicator which can be used on days of light wind – the wind itself. When a thermal bubble lifts off, air has to flow in to replace it, and, if the prevailing wind is only light, then these movements are strong enough to affect its direction or even cancel it out altogether. In crude terms this means that a sudden calm spell on a day of gentle breeze usually means a thermal lifting off upwind (in terms of the prevailing wind direction); sometimes the effect is strong enough to completely reverse the wind direction for a minute or two. Similarly an increase in strength means a thermal generating downwind, if the wind comes more from the right the thermal is on the left and so on.

The change in wind direction does not give any indication of the distance or scale of the lift, just its direction. It could be a very large disturbance a mile or more away, or a much smaller one a lot closer. However, knowing the direction to search in gives an invaluable start, and all experienced R/C thermal pilots will have a light wool or mylar streamer flying from their transmitter aerial to indicate any wind shifts. If the streamer shifts, believe it and fly in that direction. Many more times than not you will contact lift.

Days with stronger winds are much more difficult, but it is still possible to detect thermal induced changes in wind direction. It is also worth watching the direction of fall of the bungee parachute after it has been released from the model, and its *rate* of descent. If this seems slower than normal, or is at an angle to what appears to be the prevailing wind, this can again be evidence of lift.

Another good indicator is the behaviour of the model on the towline or bungee. In order to exploit this, the pilot must be absolutely familiar with the way in which the model climbs on the line in 'neutral' air at the particular wind speed which is blowing. If launching into an area of lift,

the climb will be more rapid and the model will have a tighter and more lively feel about it on the towline. A stronger dive will also be needed at the top in order to persuade the tow ring to release, and the subsequent zoom will be more energetic and climb higher. If this happens, it is worth circling back straight from the top of the launch. Beware the situation where the model starts up the launch as if in lift, but then sags towards the top of the line. This is indicative of an area of lift which has just passed through and which is being followed by the inevitable area of sink. In such cases a quick decision is required – either turn back to get to the thermal which has just passed through or punch forward to look for the next one coming downwind.

If the model is being hand towed by a clubmate, and he is sufficiently experienced, he will be easily able to recognise the difference in behaviour if it is being towed through lift. Instead of hanging back, as is normal for even the best adjusted model on a 150-metre towline, the sailplane will tend to pull straight overhead, and

Another well known competitor in multi-task events is Dave Worral, seen here in a windswept Welsh field.

it is worth arranging a signal to be made by the tow man in such circumstances.

Almost as important as detecting lift is detecting, and avoiding, **sink**. Since what goes up must come down, every area of lift has its corresponding area of sinking air. In fact, many developed thermals are completely surrounded by an area of sink. Signs to watch out for from the ground are a sudden temporary increase in wind speed (associated with the thermal being downwind and the cold infill air rushing in), a degree or two drop in temperature and a reluctance of the model to climb properly on tow. In any of these circumstances, either delay launching until things improve or, if already on tow, once free of the line fly away as rapidly as possible from the area.

If the model is flying free, and is not in any apparent lift, the next thing to do is to set up a search pattern over one of the favoured areas. When searching for lift it is useless to fly directly overhead, the model needs to be some distance away horizontally so that disturbances to the flight path can be noted, as it is these disturbances which give more clues as to the presence of lift. There is no substitute here for experience with the model; the more flying the pilot has done with a particular sailplane, the more familiar he will be with the way it normally flies and the easier it will be to spot any disturbances to this. Most lift cores are surrounded by an area of turbulence, so if a model which has been flying smoothly suddenly starts to jump about, it may well indicate the presence of a thermal in the immediate area. In particular, if the model is pushed hard one way, it is worth turning back equally hard into the rising wing and flying in that direction, as lift will often push a model away in this manner.

The benefits of flying at a distance will become apparent when the model does enter lift, as the bodily upward displacement of the model, coupled with a slight increase in flying speed will be much easier to observe.

Exploiting lift

Once convinced that the model has entered an area of rising air, the immediate thing to do is to circle. Most pilots favour one hand or the other, but it is worth putting in the practice to ensure that the model can be circled either clockwise or anti-clockwise as the situation dictates with equal comfort. The key thing to do at this stage is to watch the model like a hawk and assess exactly what it is doing. Is it going up? If so fine, keep circling. Is it coming down? If so, break out of the circle and fly away at an angle to the wind to resume the search pattern. Is it just about holding its own? If so **keep circling**. It is amazing how often a model will struggle, just holding the same height for the first minute or two and then suddenly start to climb away.

Once the model is climbing in the lift, do not be content to simply let it go where it wishes, keep on top of it and keep flying it, and, above all, observe which side of the circle seems to be giving the best climb rate. Move the model gradually in that direction by translating the circle into an oval or race-track pattern, and keep moving it about carefully within the rising air until it is established in the strongest part of the lift.

By this time the model will probably be going downwind. Just how far to go downwind in a thermal is a matter of personal judgement based upon knowledge of the ability of the particular model to penetrate back upwind, the eyesight and confidence of the pilot and the rate at which it is climbing. Never forget that the glider will probably have to fly back through some of the sink associated with the thermal and allow for this when deciding the point of no return. A good rule of thumb is to constantly assess the *angle* which the model is making with the horizon. If this angle is steadily increasing, then, all other things being equal, it is safe to continue downwind with the lift. If the angle is just staying the same it is time to consider getting back, and if the angle is decreasing it is *definitely* time to get back.

If the model starts getting too high for comfort, use the air brakes if you have them. If you do not have brakes, then add some down trim to speed the model up a little and fly it away from the lift in a straight line. If you are having difficulty seeing the model due to excessive height, avoid sharp turns and sudden control movements, just keep it going with down trim and fly away from the lift.

Should one always circle when in lift? The answer to this is "almost always", but there are areas of lift which do not move back as one might expect with the wind. One such is the wave lift mentioned in Chapter 4; here a tacking flight path to and fro is required to keep within the lift, if the model is circled back it will drop out of the back of the wave and probably be too low to get back into it. Another form of stationary lift sometimes observed, especially in rather windier conditions, is a bolster generated by a small valley or sunken area, as shown in Figure 4.4 (on page 21). Here again, circling will lose the lift.

After leaving a thermal to fly back upwind, the time to look for lift is while there is still plenty of height in hand; it is a fact that thermals grow in both size and strength as they rise, so it is easier to find lift at 800 feet than it is at 400 feet. When leaving lift downwind of the flying field it is a good policy to exit from one side of the thermal and fly back up one side or the other of the field, rather than coming straight back upwind towards the pilot. This has the advantage of presenting the model at a better angle to judge the air it is flying through, and also gives the best chance of avoiding the sink which will almost certainly be following the thermal downwind.

On a decent day, it is possible to exploit one thermal after another, and on a really good day flights of two hours and more are not uncommon. Actually, these longer flights can become rather wearing, especially if most of the time the glider is at great height. In my club, one can always tell when the weather looks really good as the folding chairs appear on the field in anticipa-

The pilot of this clean-looking 100S model is just receiving his transmitter from his timekeeper.

tion of the need to rest the legs and ease the neck muscles! On one memorable day last year, no less than 13 flights of between one and two hours were made, and two of between two and three. Such conditions usually only occur once or twice a year, but the sense of satisfaction in making a twenty-minute flight when everybody else is having difficulty doing ten is just as great.

In the early stages, the newcomer, even after he has mastered the art of actually flying his model, will think that the more experienced thermal pilots have either entered a pact with the devil, or are blessed with a sixth sense, as they will seem to find lift over and over again while the beginner, flying in the same area of sky, is just gliding down from line height for five or six minute flights. The secret is to persist, follow the experts and stick with them when they start circling. At first, really strong lift will be needed to be obvious, but gradually the ability to recognise the subtle changes in model performance which

*Mind the goal posts! A 100S model on the base
leg of its approach for landing.*

take place when it is flirting with even light lift
will be acquired. Stick at it, watch the transmitter
streamer and act on it, watch for birds, watch the
other models, it will get easier.

It is important not to get carried away, literally, by the first big thermal encountered; it is
very easy to let ambition outweigh eyesight, and
many good thermal soaring models have been
lost either straight upwards or at long distances
downwind. Work up gradually to the really high
climbs and long flights.

On the subject of landing. Landing a thermal
soarer on a flat field in reasonable wind conditions is quite straightforward, as none of the
problems of turbulence and rough ground which
plague the slope soarer are evident. However,
most contests require a precision or spot landing,
so it is worthwhile to always take the opportunity to practise. There is a technique to landing at
a precise time and place, as is required in contests, and it works as follows.

With one minute to go to the nominated landing time, the model should be flying upwind, 30
or 40 yards out to one side of the pilot and level
with him, at about 100 feet high. When it is 20 to
30 yards upwind, it is turned across wind and
flown to a point 30 or forty yards on the other
side of the pilot, who should be standing directly

upwind of the landing spot. With about 40 seconds to go the model is turned and flown downwind, shedding height by careful use of elevator
and/or air brakes. When 30 or 40 yards downwind of the pilot it is turned and flown across
wind, and then turned into the final approach at
about 20 feet high and, most importantly, with
15 seconds to go. The model is then either held
back by slowing it with up elevator, or pushed on
with down, height is adjusted with the air brakes
and it is flown straight in to the landing spot,
where it will arrive just a second or two short of
the nominated time.

The approach has to be adjusted a little to take
account of wind strength, but once worked out
for a particular set of conditions it works every
time, and is much better than simply whizzing
around in a series of turns and landing any old
how.

To the casual observer watching a group of
thermal pilots flying it may appear a little tame –
no aerobatics, no high speed low runs, just gentle
circling and moving about the sky. However,
thermal soaring is very much a participant sport,
and the level of concentration required to fly
well is well known to all those who take part, as
is the great satisfaction that is obtained from a
flight well performed.

CHAPTER 14

PSS models

As briefly mentioned in earlier chapters, the branch of slope soaring which involves flying scale or near-scale models of powered aircraft is commonly referred to as PSS – Power Slope Scale – to differentiate it from the more traditional form of scale glider flying where models are of full-size sailplanes.

PSS is a relatively recent development in soaring and has attracted devotees from the ranks of both glider and power radio control enthusiasts. In consequence, and due to the rather different airframes which must be built, many of the techniques used in PSS design and construction are more akin to those commonly used by radio power modellers. Indeed, many PSS projects started life as powered designs, and the hundreds of scale plans for powered aircraft available from many sources form a very useful pool of designs, many of which may be converted for PSS use. However, to some extent PSS is in front of power scale developments in that ducted fan and (lately) genuine turbine powered replicas of jet aircraft are only just coming to prominence and – a severe drawback as far as the average modeller is concerned – they are very expensive, extremely complex and require 'hard-top' runways for satisfactory operation.

For the jet enthusiast of limited means or ability PSS offers a way to fly quite convincing replicas of the latest jet aircraft without mortgaging the house. Those familiar with present-day full-size military and civil jets will be puzzled - surely these aeroplanes are totally unsuitable for glider models? Certainly, any loss of power in the real thing does not inspire a desire in the driver to stay seated! This is where the skill of the PSS designer comes in. Subtle stretching of wing area, reductions in fuselage cross-section, incorporation of efficient soaring wing sections such as E205, S3021 or any of the later fast sections intended for F3B and F3J use, fairing in drag-producing intakes and so on can produce a model which, while it may be really stand-off or even semi-scale, can be totally convincing in the air. The illusion is usually aided by the use of scale colour schemes and markings plus surface detailing.

However, it is not just jet aircraft which form the staple diet of the PSS designer – World War 2 fighters are popular and, due to their layout, can be built virtually 100% scale. Prop-driven transport aircraft such as the DC3 and Constellation, bombers like the Lancaster and B29, in fact almost any reasonably clean full-size prototype

Two good examples of WW2 PSS
subjects – a late mark of Spitfire *and a*
P51B. *Models such as these fly like
good non-scale sport aerobatic slope
soarers.*

can be recreated for PSS in sizes ranging from a couple of feet wing span up to vast airframes spanning as much as sixteen or more feet.

The latest aviation magazines will provide a continuing source of three-views to inspire the design of PSS models, and there are also many really excellent coffee-table style reference books with full colour drawings. If the modeller has, or knows someone who has, a large collection of back issues of the *Aeromodeller* magazine, especially those dating from the 1950s, 1960s and 1970s, he will find these a fertile source of three-views of suitable PSS subjects. Some modellers seek out ever more 'off-the-wall' designs, and some even specialise in building models of project aircraft which never saw the light of day as full-size airframes. A search through one of the books which details the fascinating projects created by the German aircraft manufacturers during the latter part of World War 2 will reveal many offbeat and attractive shapes which can be built as PSS models, often proving the validity of the layout of the never-completed full size.

There is even a sub-division of PSS which encompasses the building of scale (usually 1:1)

models of soaring birds! Some of these have to cheat a little by employing transparent fins etc., as the models lack the totally mobile wings and on-board computer (i.e. brain!) of the originals, but they can be amusing and look quite convincing in flight.

Constructionally, although some PSS types are built using traditional balsa structures, the more complex fuselage shapes found in jet aircraft have encouraged the development of simpler airframes. These often consist of a basic balsa box fuselage which contains the radio equipment and provides hard mounting points for the wing and tail surfaces, clad in a selection of hot-wire cut blue or white foam fairings to reproduce the desired cross-sections. A surface skin of wrapping paper, applied with thinned PVA glue or heat-shrink film, is usually employed – even gummed parcel tape can be satisfactorily used. The wings are normally conventional balsa or veneer skinned foam cored units, less commonly a traditional built-up wing may be used, and tail surfaces are, in the main, simple all-solid balsa types.

It is normal for the smaller and simpler models to use just aileron and elevator controls, while

(A)

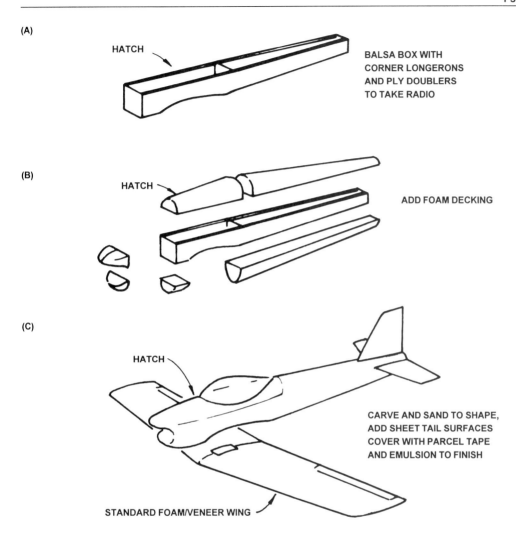

HATCH

BALSA BOX WITH
CORNER LONGERONS
AND PLY DOUBLERS
TO TAKE RADIO

(B)

HATCH

ADD FOAM DECKING

(C)

HATCH

CARVE AND SAND TO SHAPE,
ADD SHEET TAIL SURFACES
COVER WITH PARCEL TAPE
AND EMULSION TO FINISH

STANDARD FOAM/VENEER WING

Figure 14.1 *Basic PSS structure.*

rudder, working flaps and air brakes etc. are found on bigger designs. Almost without exception, prototypes which have retractable undercarriages are chosen and no undercarriage is fitted to the model. The average slope site landing area is not conducive to landing a model fitted with wheels, let alone one fitted with an easily damaged retractable undercarriage, so the model is created in the 'wheels up' form which looks right in the air, and belly landed like a normal slope soarer.

When it comes to flying a PSS model, the level of skill required really depends to a large extent upon the prototype. Since they are mostly aileron controlled models, some experience with an ordinary aileron slope soarer is needed, but given this many of the WW2 fighter and less extreme jet types handle just like any other aileron slope

Stewart Bennett gives Brian Lord's PSS **Canberra** *a vigorous send-off. The model is modified from a Nexus plan originally intended as a power model, but performs well on the slope.*

model. Due to the fact that the need to produce the maximum amount of lift from relatively small wings dictates the use of soaring rather than aerobatic sections, PSS models normally perform manoeuvres in the fashion of the prototype i.e. fast, open loops and rolls, rather than the full aerobatic repertoire of a specialist slope aerobatic model. There are exceptions to this, and models of clean straight-wing piston fighters, such as the Mustang, can be created to virtually copy the lay-out of a slope aerobatic type, with the appropriate performance. However, as with most scale flying, the challenge is to realistically emulate the performance of the full-size prototype.

Most PSS models – there are exceptions such as the Lockheed U2 which, with its huge high aspect ratio wing can soar as well as most scale sailplanes – will require decent lift to perform convincingly. This means choosing a good site, and flying them when there is a reasonable wind blowing straight onto the face. If flown in marginal conditions where they can only just remain airborne, the authenticity of the flight pattern suffers and the models become tricky and difficult to fly. More than with most other types it is necessary to keep the flying speed of a PSS model up, so that crisp control responses are main-

tained. Some of the more extreme modern jet layouts have strange aerodynamic habits – hardly surprising under the circumstances – and are tricky in flight. In particular, models featuring extremes of wing sweep have to be watched since, even if they are travelling well above what would be the normal stalling speed, heavy handed application of elevator control can cause huge and instant increases in drag and dramatic loss of air speed, followed by loss of control. Delta wing types are even more susceptible to this since large changes of pitch angle will present the whole of the wing area to the airflow, acting like one great air brake.

The correct technique with a typical PSS model is to push it out from a fast level launch and constantly convert the lift into forward speed rather than letting it balloon upwards. When making turns, these should be made wide

Nice C-47 *shows how convincing larger PSS models can be. Simple foam and balsa construction and plain but well executed finish with just enough detail.*

Close encounter of the PSS kind! Stewart Bennett's A-10 **Warthog** *ground attack aircraft comes close to scoring a kill! This model is scratch-built to Stewart's own design using foam shapes covered, for the most part, with computer paper.*

and sweeping, with minimum of up elevator input, in order to conserve flying speed. Looping manoeuvres should be approached in the same fashion, first picking up plenty of excess air speed in a shallow dive and then flying the model around the loop with small elevator movements, so that speed is maintained. Rolls are much less of a problem with the average PSS model as, with relatively short wings and fairly powerful ailerons, the roll rate is usually pretty rapid if required. However, due to the use of a largely flat-bottomed wing section, rolls, especially consecutive rolls, may need careful attention to applying down elevator in the inverted portion to keep them nice and axial – but once again the watchword is caution since too much down will quickly rob the model of air speed. Once again, due to the type of wing section normally used, the inverted flight performance of many PSS models will not be particularly good, unless, that

is, they are being operated in very good lift indeed. Even in these circumstances, it is very easy to cause the model to enter an inverted stall, which is not something one would want to do if too close to the slope.

One useful technique which can help if conditions are a little marginal, is to build a catapult hook into the model and launch it via a short, relatively strong bungee. This is also of assistance in cases where the shape of the model makes it awkward to grasp firmly for a normal hand launch. The extra energy imparted by the bungee gives the best possible chance of settling into the lift area. The question of models being difficult to hand launch can also be addressed by providing special grips and recesses in the fuselage for the launcher's fingers. This is not something which should be ignored, especially with the larger models, as trying to launch an aeroplane with a smooth ten inch diameter completely circular fuselage (e.g. a Valiant, B36 or similar) while being buffeted on the edge of a hill by a twenty-knot wind can be quite a disturbing experience.

A word of caution about flying in company with several other PSS models, as would be the case at one of the increasingly popular PSS fly-ins. If a number of models of different types are flying on the slope, they tend to use different parts of the sky – lightweights will be high above the slope; big, efficient scale gliders high up and far out; trainer types using the lift sufficiently far from the slope face for safety; and pylon race types dashing back and forth close in. However, if six or more PSS models are flying together, they will all be seeking the area of maximum lift to enable them to fly smoothly and quickly, and will tend to be compressed into a relatively small band of air in front of the ridge. In such circumstances, a very sharp watch needs to be kept to avoid mid-air collisions, which are, in fact, quite a common occurrence at PSS fly-ins. These vary from simple touching of wing tips to full-blown head-on affairs resulting in the total destruction of one or both models. If you don't want to take

111

the risk, it is best to keep your model on the ground in these circumstances.

PSS can be a lot of fun; models can be built from inexpensive materials and, despite the battering which a slope soarer usually takes, they can be made to last for a long time as there is no fuel seepage or engine vibration and nothing to wear out. The best PSS models are as convincing in appearance, even close up, as a good non-flying plastic kit, with cockpit detail, excellent surface detailing etc., but even quite a plain and simply finished model can look really good in the air if it is well flown in the manner of the prototype.

CHAPTER 15

Scale sailplanes

In contrast to the PSS scale models discussed in the last chapter, this chapter is concerned with models of subjects which are sailplanes or gliders in their full-size incarnations. Anyone who has any interest at all in soaring, powerless flight must be impressed by the sight of a modern full-size glassfibre high-performance sailplane in flight. Their effortless grace and seeming ability to defy gravity makes them one of the most spectacular and impressive of all flying machines.

In the model world, there are available quarter scale or even larger representations of such sailplanes using essentially the same materials and construction techniques as the full size, albeit somewhat simplified. These models are often almost-ready-to-fly, requiring only installation of the equipment and setting up. Needless to say, the cost of such a model is prohibitive for many enthusiasts, although those who have flown these big, commercially produced 'glass ships' rave about their performance from slope or towline.

For the enthusiast who does not mind doing his own building, there is a cheaper alternative route which can produce almost as good results as those obtained by the big all-moulded models. Many fibreglass shell fuselages are available from numerous sources for scale gliders ranging from $1/6$ scale upwards, and flying surfaces produced in the conventional way from polystyrene foam cores skinned with balsa or veneer, incorporating hardwood or composite spars, mated to one of these fuselages can result, albeit at the expense of some considerable labour, in a flying machine every bit as spectacular in appearance and performance as an all-moulded model costing many hundreds of pounds. Even going the DIY route, a $1/4$ or $1/3$ scale sailplane spanning upwards of four metres is going to be a relatively expensive undertaking, although these larger sizes reward the time and money invested in them with great realism of flying performance. Smaller scale models of modern sailplanes can still be quite satisfying; a $1/5$ scale model of a 15 metre standard class glider, spanning three metres, is big enough to be an efficient and realistic soarer, but below this scale, the very high aspect ratios found in modern glass sailplanes tend to reduce the wing chord of $1/6$ to $1/8$ scale replicas to the level where inefficiency and poor handling characteristics (tip stalling) can be expected.

The situation is rather different with the older style of glider, in particular big two-seat trainers such as the Slingsby T-21 and Tandem Tutor as,

Quarter scale Olympia 2B *in balsa and wood.*

with their relatively low aspect ratios and large wing areas, quite sensible models result at $^1/_6$ to $^1/_8$ scale factors. The classic wooden gliders built from the mid 1930s through to the start of the fibreglass revolution in the 1960s, culminating in such elegant types as the *Olympia* and *Slingsby Skylark*, are ideal choices for the modeller who wishes to build a model using traditional balsa and ply constructional techniques, and very successful models can be built in all scales. Going back even further, some of the (often idiosyncratic) very early gliders from the 1920s and the 'primary' trainer types from the 1930s make fascinating modelling challenges, and while their relatively low efficiency tends to limit their performance to slope soaring in good lift, they can be most appealing in flight, as well as providing hours of interesting building in the workshop.

Most, if not all, of the advice on construction, radio installation and flying in the earlier chapters applies as much to scale model sailplanes as it does to any other type. One area where extra thought is required, however, is in producing a finish which gives that added air of realism to the scale model.

The RTF glassfibre models carry their own finish built into the glassfibre resin. The vast majority of modern sailplanes are finished in more or less plain white with just a little colour trim, and most of the commercial models are finished like this to a very high standard requiring only the application of small areas of spray trim and possibly registration letters and club badges etc. to complete a realistic finish. Being 'moulded in',

the finish is also quite durable, although anyone who has paid the price required to obtain one of these beautiful models will want to have some form of protective sleeving or carrying case to prevent the lovely finish being scratched during transportation. Unfortunately, white, while a natural choice for a full-size high-performance sailplane, is not the first choice for a model which is going to be flown high and far away from the operator. As was discussed in an earlier chapter, a dark coloured underside with a light coloured top surface is the best combination for a model, but very few full-size gliders feature such a colour scheme.

For a home-built replica of a glassfibre glider, there is absolutely no doubt that an epoxy glass finish on the flying surfaces, coupled with a glassfibre shell fuselage, and the whole spray painted will give the best representation of the full-size finish. However, with care, a very good job can be done with plastic film covering on the flying surfaces. When it comes to painting the fuselage to match, the modeller will soon discover that there are more shades of the humble colour white than he ever thought possible! The only real way to guarantee a good match is to use paint marketed by the film manufacturer and keyed to match his film colour.

The very early gliders were usually covered in plain varnished fabric, which can be very well represented by either heat-shrink nylon fabric covering, or, on smaller models, tissue or tissue over mylar. The most attractive and varied colour schemes are found in the gliders of the mid

1930s onwards, until the appearance of the predominantly all-white glass aircraft in the 1960s. Since these sailplanes were usually of built-up construction with planked or moulded ply fuselages and fabric-covered flying surfaces finished in cellulose dope, exactly the same materials can be used on the scale replica to produce a perfectly authentic appearance. The fabric can be either nylon or silk, or one of the heat-shrink fabrics, and coloured areas can be represented with cellulose spray painting.

Thanks to the efforts of a number of enthusiasts (at least one of these gentlemen also being a keen and prolific builder of models) and such organisations as the Vintage Glider Club, there are now quite a large number of lovingly restored vintage sailplanes from the 1920s onwards flying again. The opportunity therefore exists to obtain first-hand photographs and carry out a detailed inspection of the subject of many proposed models by visiting the appropriate gliding site.

One area in which economies should not be made when building a large scale sailplane (or equipping a moulded model) is that of the radio equipment, in particular the servos. These models have large flying surfaces, and the modern models in particular can fly at very high speeds and hence place large loads on the servos. The normal plastic-geared variety, perfectly adequate for most applications, can be suspect in such situations, and particularly for the mini or micro servos often installed inside wings for aileron and flap operation, it is wise to make the extra investment required to obtain metal-geared servos with ball-raced output gears.

There is absolutely no reason why any reasonable sized scale model (say $^1/_6$ scale or bigger) should require any non-scale aerodynamic amendments, such as enlarged tail surfaces, to produce a perfectly satisfactory flying model. The sole exception to this is in the area of wing sections for the older gliders, which often used thick and very highly cambered (and hence high-drag) one speed sections. Particularly for a model

used for slope soaring, where flying in quite strong winds is the norm, this type of section can lead to an embarrassing lack of ability to penetrate into wind. In such cases designers often substitute a 'faster' more modern section, but as these are usually much thinner than the original, great care is required to avoid losing the essential character of the sailplane, producing what is really a semi-scale model. A similar problem, but with different causes, can afflict models of the most modern sailplanes; in this case the original will use a laminar flow type of section i.e. one which relies for its performance on keeping the airflow attached to the surface of the section over virtually the full wing chord. In order to achieve this attachment, very high standards of surface accuracy and finish are necessary, and these can only really be guaranteed in model replicas by the use of moulded construction and large ($^1/_4$ or $^1/_3$) scale. A scale replica of a full-size laminar flow section inaccurately reproduced will not operate in the correct fashion – the airflow will detach and become turbulent as is the case with 'normal' sections. A laminar flow wing operating in this way will be very inefficient and produce a disappointing performance.

The question of minimum practicable size (scale) for a modern replica has already been touched upon. To explain this a little further, consider the fact that a $^1/_5$ scale model of even a large 'open' class modern sailplane will have a wing chord at the tip of only a few inches. In this kind

Beautifully detailed **Elfe S-4** *glass scale sailplane by John Gottschalk.*

Elegant gull wing **Reiher** *is quite small scale and flies well from the towline.*

of size, the laws of aerodynamics are strongly against us, and in extreme circumstances the wing will produce more drag than lift! In general terms, any scale which will result in a tip chord of less than four inches should be avoided, although this does depend to some extent upon the wing planform. For example, an aircraft such as the Discus with a multi-tapered planform (typical of many of the very latest) can probably be successfully built with a smaller tip chord than a type which has a straight root-to-tip taper.

Given sensible construction which has produced a model with weight and wing loading within normally acceptable limits, any decent scale model will be just as easy to fly from the slope as a non-scale model of similar size and loading. By its nature, a scale model will normally use ailerons as the primary directional control, and some experience with a non-scale aileron model is useful before flying your scale replica. The other point to watch is that, with the higher aspect ratio modern gliders, a large degree

of aileron differential movement is often needed i.e. the upgoing aileron (on the downgoing wing) should move through a greater angle than the downgoing aileron (on the upgoing wing) which can be arranged either by adjusting the geometry of the aileron linkage, or, if using a computer radio, via the programming adjustments on the transmitter. Failure to arrange this may result in an adverse yaw condition, with the model initially yawing in the opposite direction to the applied aileron. Although this can be countered by applying rudder (if the pilot is not well versed in flying separate aileron and rudder controls, coupling of the aileron and rudder functions is a good idea, at least for first flights) it does result in untidy and unrealistic flying, and can also have a more serious side effect in that the downgoing aileron, especially on the narrow tip-chord wings found on scale models, can promote a tip stall which will cause the model to drop off into a spin in the opposite direction to the applied aileron. Until thoroughly familiar with the model, it is sensible to restrict flying to slope soaring on 'good' slopes in conditions which are known to produce strong and consistent lift – this is a comment which could be applied to any new slope soarer.

Flying a scale model from a towline does require a little care during the launch phase since, although ailerons may be the primary turn

Close-up of Bob Goldman's **Olympia 2B** *shows beautiful finish.*

control, any attempt to use them to correct divergence from a straight line on the tow can produce unexpected responses due to the high angle of attack and peculiar lift regime in which the model operates during the tow launch. Normal practice is to keep the tow straight using rudder control and revert to ailerons once off the line. Indeed, models, not just scale models but aileron equipped thermal soarers, which fly with coupled aileron and rudder controls, often have the coupling switched out via the transmitter mixer during the towing phase so that the rudder may be used independently.

Contests for scale sailplanes are, at least in this country, mostly run as slope soaring events. Rules vary, but normally the emphasis is placed on flying, with static judging being restricted to the stand-off format where the model is judged from a few yards distance rather than minutely examined as is often the case with power scale models. Very often the entry is split into two classes, modern and vintage; while the ways of defining this split vary, the more usual one is to include any replicas of 'glass ships' in the modern section and everything else in vintage. Sometimes a cut-off date is used which results in some of the advanced wooden gliders (such as the later *Slingsby Skylark*) or metal sailplanes (like the *Blanik*) being included with the fibreglass designs in the modern class.

The actual flying tests usually involve a flight demonstrating the model in the fashion of the full size, sometimes a precision landing and often a short cross-country test. Actually, the highly efficient large scale glassfibre models make very good competitive types for use in full-blown cross-country contests in competition with non-scale types. The only real drawback to using them in this capacity is the risk involved in flying an expensive model, or one which has consumed a lot of building hours, at the extremes of distance and in poor lift conditions which are often a fact of life in cross-country flying. If the modeller can steel himself to live with this, then the big

scale model has, in normal conditions, as much chance of doing well in a cross-country contest as any specialist type.

There are usually only a few meetings each year on flat-field sites for scale sailplanes, but most of these offer the option of aerotowed launches by suitable tug power models. Given the appropriate release mechanism in the glider, this is a thrilling and realistic way of operating a scale sailplane, and very long thermal flights are possible from the high launches obtained. The tugs available usually use big engines to give them the muscle to comfortably tow the largest scale sailplanes. Power winches are also used at some of these meetings but are less popular than aerotowing, having a tendency to produce some rather uncomfortable and potentially damaging moments on launch for those who are not fully familiar with the technique.

A type of aircraft which has gained ground steadily in the full-size world over the last ten years has been the motor glider – or self-launching sailplane. Many of the earlier examples of these had fairly woeful performances compared with their pure glider contemporaries. I recall asking a friend who had a part-share in such a machine what it was like to fly. After giving the matter some thought, he replied "Well, it is a pretty b***** awful powered aircraft". After a

Martin Simon's gorgeous ¼ scale gull wing PWS101.

117

Grunau Baby *by Frank Smith with a 'V' tailed scale aerobatic glider in the background.*

pause he continued "But come to think of it, it is a pretty b***** awful glider too!". Clearly a case of having the worst of both worlds! The more modern motor gliders are much better in all departments and the best of them are very effective soaring machines once the fan is turned off. It follows that they also make very effective models, the only unfortunate feature being the need to incorporate a noisy, messy IC engine. However, all is not lost, as electric power has progressed to a stage of efficiency where a quarter scale motor glider replica can be produced with a very adequate electric power system. Admittedly, this usually involves the use of one of the more expensive high-efficiency motors, but the advantages of quiet, clean operation, not to mention the ability to start and stop the motor at will during the flight, make it well worth considering.

Smaller motor glider scale models are also a very practical proposition – there is at least one kit currently on the market for a fifty inch replica which uses an inexpensive direct-drive 400 size motor and miniature radio equipment to produce a charming, silent and thoroughly practical sport-scale model, suitable for operation from virtually any football-field size patch of grass.

There is absolutely no doubt about the attraction of a well-produced scale flying model aircraft; even the most functional of enthusiasts suffers from the urge to build and fly one at some stage. Where the scale sailplane gains over its IC powered opposite number is that, operationally, an exact scale replica is much more likely to be able to very nearly match the flying performance of the freelance, non-scale equivalent, thereby delivering the double satisfaction of a scale appearance and outstanding flying, factors which make the scale glider well worth the extra effort involved in its production.

CHAPTER 16

Self-launching sailplanes

Mention has already been made in the previous chapter of self-launching scale models – motor gliders. However, this method of flying what is basically a soaring glider is not restricted to scale models, far from it.

For many years I enjoyed flying gliders from flat fields equipped with small diesel or glow-plug engines, either mounted in the nose of the model or on a separate, detachable power pylon. While this is a perfectly satisfactory way of getting a glider up to a height where it can be used to explore for lift like a normal soaring model, it is not proposed to cover this type of auxiliary sailplane in this book. The reasons for this can be summarised as: noise, mess and incompatibility with people flying gliders on the same field!

However, there is now a practical alternative available which finds ready acceptance on the most noise-sensitive sites and usually fits in well with the operation of pure gliders given sensible co-operation – electric power.

Electric powered radio control models are not something new, however, the steady development of both motors and batteries has now reached a stage where an off-the-shelf power package is readily available for any size of radio controlled soaring model from HLG (60 inch)

upwards. Motors range from inexpensive ferrite types, with or without gearboxes, up through the more expensive ones with rare earth magnets to very expensive but powerful and maintenance-free brushless types, and are available in sizes to suit all models. A wide range of excellent folding airscrews, ideal for powered sailplanes as they permit a glide configuration almost as clean as an ordinary glider, is commercially available as are all the other requirements such as electronic switches, speed controllers and batteries.

The only soaring class of electric model recognised at international level, known by the code F5B, is a rather specialised type. Variations limited to seven and ten cell battery packs as well as an open class where the battery is simply limited to a maximum weight are flown, and the contest consists of a combined distance and duration flight. The rules have produced models which have, even in the lower cell classes, ballistic rates of climb. The typical F5B model will be around 2 metres span, will have ailerons and be (in thermal soaring terms) very heavily loaded. It will most likely feature composite moulded construction and it will be clean, efficient and fly very fast. Although these models are exciting they are definitely not suitable for beginners and do not

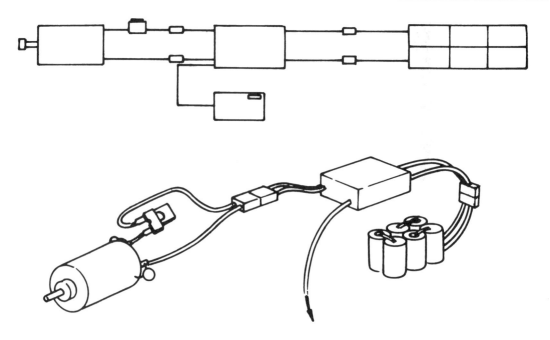

Figure 16.1 *Basic wiring of motor system.*

really fall within my definition of self-launching soaring models.

Much more likely to appeal to the average club member for regular sport thermal soaring is the national class known as E-Slot; in this class models are required to perform three 10-minute flights from one charge of the flight battery, with a maximum of 75 seconds power run each flight. The need to allow for 3¾ minutes of power from the battery acts as an automatic limit on the current at which the motor can be operated, thus limiting the rate of climb available. However, E-Slot models can still climb to towline height (150 metres) at least twice during the 75-second allotment and can hence be quite heavily loaded and fast flying. The other contest class commonly flown in the UK is the smaller E400, restricted to the cheap and freely available standard 400 size motors with again a ten minute maximum flight time, but this time allowing two minutes of motor run and recharging batteries between flights.

As the specified motor is only capable of sustained running at around 10 or 11 amps without burning out, the amount of power available is automatically limited. Models of this class are between 60 and 80 inches span and weigh 20 to 30 ounces depending upon the gearbox ratio used, producing pleasant small-field sport soarers. Both E-Slot and E400 models are restricted to a seven cell maximum battery pack (8.4 volts nominal).

While many of the electric soarers flown on club fields comply with either the E-Slot or E400 rules, many more do not, using a variety of motors and battery packs from six to ten cells. One thing which most of these models have in common is that they fall into what is known on the continent as the 'soft-fly' category – models which have relatively gentle rates of climb and are principally flown as thermal soarers with the advantage of self-launching – no bungees to lay out and no need for someone to tow the model for you.

*Modelhaus **Ninja** is typical of the type of model flown in the F5B electric class; this is a ten cell model, but open class versions use up to 30 cells for ballistic performance.*

The design layout of an electric soarer needs to differ from that of a normal thermal soarer only in so far as provision needs to be made to accommodate the motor and the flight battery. The nose of the model can be proportioned to fit the spinner of the folding airscrew being used so that when the blades are folded a clean nose entry is produced. As far as battery placement is concerned, the main thing to remember is to arrange the weighty flight battery so that in the event of a hard landing (the term most modellers use to describe a crash) there is no delicate electronic equipment positioned in front of it to act as an expensive stop!

While the general structural requirements need be little different from a thermal model of the same size (HLG to 2 metre for 400 motors, 2 metre to 100 inch for 600 size and 120" plus for cobalts or 700 size ferrites), care needs to be taken to keep the weight of the structure down so that the extra weight of the flight battery (the motor will largely replace the nose ballast which most pure gliders need to carry) is offset and the final wing loading of the model is similar to a glider of the same size. In general, this means that while the use of a fibreglass shell fuselage is a possibility, foam wings are unlikely to be the best choice for a model such as this. With care, wing loadings of 7 to 8 ounces per square foot should be achievable for any size of electric soarer.

The actual electric power installation need not be difficult to organise. Pre-wired setups are available off-the-shelf for 600 size motors, but the wiring of a simple system is no problem for the average enthuusiast. Use flexible silicon wire and include a fuse in the circuit so that if the motor is stalled for any reason there is a safety cut-out. Battery packs are best bought pre-assembled if possible, but can be soldered up at home with care. The secret is to use a big enough soldering iron (50 watts minimum, 75 watts is better), keep everything absolutely clean and keep the iron in contact for the minimum of time necessary to make a good joint. One thing which will be needed is a battery charger capable of charging the highest voltage pack to be used at a reasonable rate – typically between 1.5 and 3.5 amps. This should run from a 12-volt source to permit field charging, but actually it is perfectly possible to enjoy a full afternoon's flying without having field charging available. My favourite class is E400 and, due to the low current demand by these motors, it is possible to use standard AA pencells instead of the more expensive AR or SCR types. This means that, at current prices, four 7-cell battery packs can be bought for less than £30 – the price of one 1700 SCR pack. With four charged packs, if there is any lift about at all, two or three hours of flying time can be achieved – enough for most people in one session!

To give some idea of the type of inexpensive setups which will work well and provide many

*This is me with my simple **Clubman** direct drive E400 for six or seven cells.*

hours of enjoyable sport soaring, there follows brief descriptions of some of my models.

The **Clubman** is a basic lightweight E400 model with the simplest and least expensive possible equipment. The power train in this 57 inch 21 ounce model is a 7.2 volt Graupner Speed 400 driving a Robbe 6" × 3.5" folding airscrew with a Robbe RSC210 electronic on/off switch. Power supply is a six-cell pack (7.2 volts) of Sanyo 600 or 700 AA cells – the total cost of the power train at current prices is less than £40. On

six cells the model is a delight to fly, giving flights of eighteen to twenty minutes without any thermal assistance. For a faster climb of shorter duration, seven cells can be used.

The **Sundancer 60** is a more refined 60 inch E400 design which uses a 7.2 volt Speed 400 with a concentric Graupner gearbox of 4:1 ratio, driving an 11" x 8" Graupner Camgear folding airscrew. Motor control is via a Tarling electronic 'soft start' switch and the battery is a seven-cell Sanyo 600 or 700 AA pack. The model weighs 26 ounces and climbs somewhat faster than the Clubman.

The **Sundancer 74** is a stretched E400 model designed specifically for contest flying to the two minute motor run rules. Power is a 6 volt Speed 400 driving a 12" x 10" Graupner Gearprop folding airscrew through a concentric 4:1 gearbox. Control is via a Graupner Picomos 18 speed controller and the battery pack in this 30 ounce model is a seven-cell Sanyo 'red' 500 AR pack, capable of delivering higher current than the 600 AA cells. The model will climb to 500 feet twice during the two minute motor run and, with the prop folded, glides and thermals like a two metre glider.

The **Sundancer 96** is an 8-foot span E-Slot model which uses a ball-raced Speed 600 ferrite motor driving a fourteen inch diameter Camgear

*Ian Dale holds my **Sundancer 74** and his own **Electron**, while Gordon John has his un-named 74 inch curved tip model and my **Sundancer 60** – all E400 class soarers.*

Gordon Johnson fits the spinner on his elegant pod and boom design.

airscrew through a 2.8:1 concentric gearbox. Control is via a Picomos 18 speed controller and the battery pack is a seven-cell Sanyo 1700 SCR. Wing loading is 8 ounces per square foot and the model soars like a good 100S thermal soarer.

The **Northern Light** is a large area, light 2 metre model which uses a 400 size, but more powerful, tuned AP29 motor driving an 11" x 8" Camgear prop via a Fanfare 3:1 single stage gearbox. Speed control is a Tarling Microstar 20 and the battery pack is a seven-cell Sanyo 1400 SC battery pack.

The **Luton Buzzard** is a 72" scale power glider, a pusher, powered by an AP29 with a Fanfare 3:1 gearbox and an 8" x 4" Graupner non-folding Slimprop. Power supply is controlled via a Picomos 18 speed controller and the battery pack is a six-cell Sanyo 1000 SC. As a scale model, with an undercarriage, this model requires rather more lift than the freelance designs, but given decent lift it will soar nicely.

The **Graupner Ultra-Fly** is a 98" model and uses an 8.4 volt Speed 600 driving a 15 inch three-bladed Graupner folding airscrew through a Master 3:1 offset gearbox. Switching is via a servo-driven double microswitch to give a soft start facility (essential when using a gearbox) and the battery is a seven-cell 1700 SCR. This model is rather heavily loaded at 11 ounces per square

foot, but is a good performer capable of flying well in quite windy conditions.

As can be seen from the above selection, plenty of variety is available in electric soarers. If more expensive cobalt motors, capable of producing high power outputs at high currents, or 700 size ferrite motors, geared or direct drive, are included almost any type of soaring model can be 'electrified'.

Flying an electric self-launching soarer is no different from flying a normal thermal soarer once the power is shut off and the propeller is folded. However, it takes a little practice to get the best out of the lower powered models during the climb phase. The secret is to avoid trying to climb the model at too steep an angle – the wing must be made to work during the climb, so initially err on the side of climbing at too shallow an angle and experiment to find out what attitude gives you the best results. Once you have been flying electric soarers for a while you will become aware of two advantages which they have over straight thermal gliders. First, the relatively gentle climb makes them very good thermal indicators during the climb phase – the increase in climb rate when flying into lift is very obvious and easy to spot. Secondly, the model has a greater level of security, at least while there is still some power in reserve, when following lift downwind – if the lift evaporates and the model has to be flown back upwind through poor air, a judicious application of power can save a landing out and a long walk.

As the structure of an electric model may be rather lighter than the average thermal soarer, some care is required in flying the model out of the strong thermals, particularly with the smaller models which rarely have air brakes. One good tip here is if a proportional speed controller is fitted rather than a simple switch, the airscrew can be used as an effective airbrake. If the throttle is just cracked open enough to cause the prop to unfold, but not so far as to produce any useful power, it will produce large quantities of drag as it windmills around. It is perfectly possible to

If electric does not appeal, a noisier and messier way is available, as on this scaled-up vintage **Lulu** *two function glider.*

build electric models every bit as strong as ordinary thermal soarers providing that care is taken in material selection and structural design.

There can be little doubt that a simple electric soarer represents one of the most convenient and practical fly-anywhere models it is possible to find. I carry one of my E400 class models in my car most of the time and often find the opportunity in the summer to slip out at lunchtime for half an hour of flying. The model can be in the air within a couple of minutes of arriving at the field – the wing is held with one bolt and the model can be carried with the all-moving tail already plugged on. A few seconds to connect the battery and switch on, a quick check of the radio and the model is away. To underline this practicality, in the course of one season, the bigger of the two Sundancer designs accumulated over 90 hours actually airborne.

The electric soarer can never completely supplant the conventional, line-launched glider, but it does provide an excellent sport model and one with which much single-handed thermal flying practice can be done. I would suggest that it is a type of model which should form part of the stable of every modeller who enjoys weekend outings on the club field.

CHAPTER 17

Vintage gliders

In recent years, nostalgia for things past has become part of most aspects of life in this country and aeromodelling is no exception. This is easy to understand when we consider that many of the thousands of people who were involved, as children and teenagers, in the explosive post-WW2 expansion of aeromodelling in the late 1940s and 1950s – the golden age of the hobby in the UK – are now reaching retirement age and have both the time and resources to either return to model flying or (as in my case) expand existing lifelong interests. The desire to recreate models which were either a part of an enjoyable youth or, in many instances, were advanced and expensive designs to which the young modeller could only aspire, is therefore understandable. What is slightly more puzzling is that much younger enthusiasts, who were not born until long after the period generally considered to be vintage in aeromodelling terms, enjoy building and flying old model aeroplane designs. The definition of vintage varies from country to country but in the UK the official cut-off date is the end of 1950 although many designs from the period up to 1956 are seen – in the US the dates are generally earlier.

There is, therefore, a healthy interest in vintage models worldwide, spearheaded in the country by the two UK 'chapters' of the Society of Antique Modellers (SAM). Many contests and rallies are held and support for these is often much greater than for contemporary contest classes. Obviously, there was very little radio flying in the vintage period and that which did take place was, in terms of modern control systems, extremely primitive. Hence the vintage movement is split broadly into two – those who like to recreate the free-flight and control-line models of their youth exactly as originally built and fly them in the same form (sometimes in competition with others), and those who are happy to apply modern radio control to suitable designs, often scaling them up or (infrequently) down for the purpose and fly them for sport and enjoyment.

Of the vintage and vintage-style models seen being flown under radio control, it must be said that gliders are in the minority. This seems strange at first sight as the glider was perhaps the most widespread type seen during the WW2 years, and for a few years thereafter, and particularly when we look outside the UK to continental Europe where medium and large size gliders suitable for radio conversion abound. However, the radio glider side of the aeromodelling hobby, perhaps more than any other, is contest-led and the constant search for better performance, involving the use of modern high-tech materials and computer developed wing sections, leaves little time for nostalgia! The British Association of Radio Control Soarers (BARCS) do run an annual league for vintage models and quite a lot of these models can be seen flown on club fields.

A vintage sailplane with radio, especially one of the bigger designs such as my **Ron Mead 1948**, which boasts 16 square feet of total area, can be an impressive and satisfying performer in lighter wind conditions. The wing sections used and general structures mean that these models are never going to compete against modern types for out-and-out performance, but, given the right conditions, they can be enormous fun to fly, with the added dimension that something historical is being created. Smaller models, such as the early A/2 class gliders (now known internationally as F1B and still the World Championship free-flight glider class – although present high aspect ratio, carbon fibre and composite models with complex multi-function tow hooks and electronic timers are a world removed from their predecessors nominally built to the same specification) are also possible using mini or micro radio gear. As an example of this, my **Jader**

*Veron **Vortex** kit model is suitable for conversion with lightweight equipment – this one is rudder only.*

60 A/2 of 1951 vintage weighs just 15 ounces complete with two-function radio – less than an ounce heavier than the free-flight original – and is a lovely little performer in light and calm conditions from slope or towline.

The vast majority of models of all types are built just for fun (referred to as sport flying) but this is even more true in the case of vintage gliders converted to R/C. If you are seeking the ultimate in performance, there is absolutely no reason to build one. However, if you enjoy building traditional wooden modelling structures and would like to produce a pretty, well-finished model with some character to fly on those calm evenings and afternoons in the summer, a vintage design with radio is worth considering.

Modifications are limited to those necessary to fit the rudder and elevator controls (as the model was originally designed to be free-flight, it should be very stable and ailerons are unlikely to be a requirement), plus judicious strengthening of areas like the wing centre section to take the

*Big **Ron Mead** vintage soarer built by John Purchase and flown by me dwarfs the 74 inch span **Sundancer** E400 – 16 square feet of total area!*

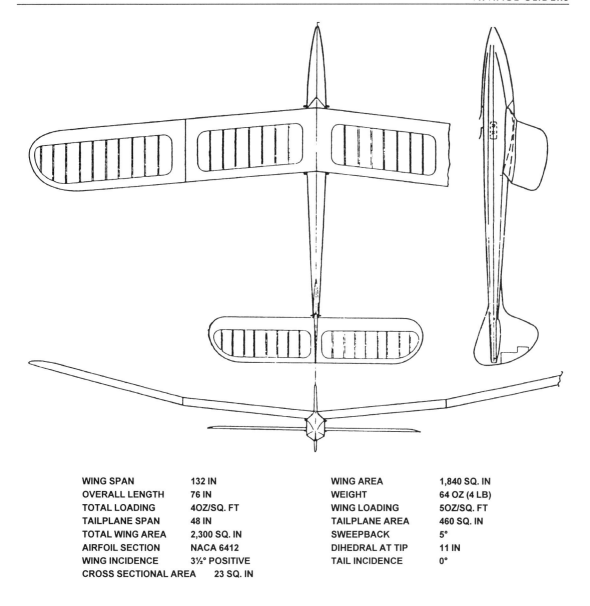

WING SPAN	132 IN	WING AREA	1,840 SQ. IN
OVERALL LENGTH	76 IN	WEIGHT	64 OZ (4 LB)
TOTAL LOADING	4OZ/SQ. FT	WING LOADING	5OZ/SQ. FT
TAILPLANE SPAN	48 IN	TAILPLANE AREA	460 SQ. IN
TOTAL WING AREA	2,300 SQ. IN	SWEEPBACK	5°
AIRFOIL SECTION	NACA 6412	DIHEDRAL AT TIP	11 IN
WING INCIDENCE	3½° POSITIVE	TAIL INCIDENCE	0°
CROSS SECTIONAL AREA	23 SQ. IN		

Figure 17.1 *G/A radio controlled glider (rudder only) by Ron Mead, Northern Heights MFC. Built to* FAI *specification.*

somewhat heavier loads likely to be imposed by radio flying. Some modellers cheat and use a modern wing section, but this really moves the model away from the true vintage conversion and if this type of model – a vintage lookalike with performance more akin to a modern light-weight soarer – is the aim, it is really better to design one from scratch. Covering and finishing

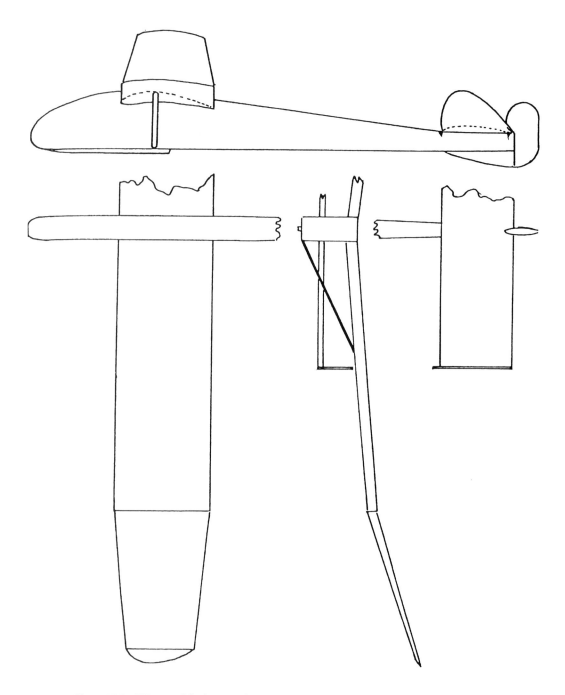

Figure 17.2   *WP 58-1 glider by R. Werler. Span 10ft, weight 6.25lb, wing loading 9.3oz/sq ft.*

Delightful twice size **Evander** *before covering shows that elegance is not the exclusive preserve of modern gliders.*

is really up to the individual. Heat-shrink fabrics are good for bigger models, alternatively traditional nylon can be used. On smaller models tissue, or one of the heat-shrink finishes that simulate tissue, is fine although my personal favourite is clear mylar with tissue on top. This gives the best of both worlds – a true vintage appearance with the benefits of extra strength. The glossy heat-shrink plastic films can be used, but these really look totally wrong and out of character on these models.

The vast majority of vintage R/C gliders are flown as thermal soaring types from bungee or tow launch on flat-field sites. Few are seen on the slopes, but they do make good slope models for the very lightest of conditions when all the more normal types are grounded due to lack of lift. The sight of a big vintage glider either wafting back and forth along the ridge top, supported by the lift produced by the merest evening drift of air from the valley below, or

climbing steadily away in a thermal on a sunny calm afternoon at the club field, is one of the most pleasant and satisfying available to an R/C glider pilot. In general, flying them is no different to flying the lighter types of modern models. You have to remember that the penetration of these designs will be limited, and, in order to respect this, the models must not be flown too far downwind as it will take a lot of time and consume a lot of height to get them back. However, when it comes to gaining height in lift, a good vintage model can match, and often surpass, many modern thermal soarers – climbing is what they do really well!

The photographs and drawings in this chapter show a few suitable subjects; however, the whole fun of vintage flying is in seeking out and recreating models that appeal to the individual, either due to some personal association, a long-cherished ambition to build a particular model or because the look of the aeroplane just appeals to the builder's aesthetic sense. Membership of one of the SAM chapters, and finding someone with an extensive collection of old modelling magazines (you will be surprised how many older modellers do have such a library) are the easiest ways to obtain three-views of suitable subjects, but the search for details of a targeted design is all part of the enjoyment for the vintage enthusiast.

As is the case with electric soarers, the vintage model is unlikely to be the only R/C glider which

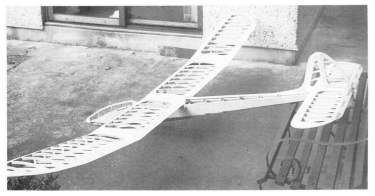

Framework of another, different version of the big **Ron Mead 1948** *design. Note the lightweight structure. My version is rather more rugged, being designed for the rigours of* BARCS *competition!*

129

a modeller owns or flies, however, having one or two vintage designs in your collection, that can be brought out and enjoyed when conditions are right, can provide a real change of pace and expand your enjoyment of this fascinating hobby, as well as providing a valuable perspective of how modern thermal soaring designs evolved from their free-flight predecessors.

CHAPTER 18

Summary

This final chapter is an attempt to pass on some of the key hints which I have picked up during more than twenty-five years of R/C gliding and forty-eight years of aeromodelling. Many of the items have been mentioned in previous chapters, but they are worth repeating here.

Choosing a model

Whether you buy RTF or build your own, it is important that the model you choose is one which you will be able to handle. Do not try to run before you can walk – a ¼ scale glassfibre sailplane or flapped multi-task model in the hands of a pilot who has only just mastered the art of keeping a rudder/elevator soarer in a straight line is an accident waiting to happen!

If you are building your own model, choose one within the scope of your building experience – a well-built, simple model is likely to fly better than a sophisticated one poorly built.

Consider the conditions in which you are likely to operate when selecting a model. If you find it unpleasant to stand on a hill in winds of twenty knots or more, a heavily loaded, fast aerobatic slope soarer is not likely to be of much use. If you live in the middle of East Anglia, any kind of slope soarer is likely to be under-employed (unless you like driving!).

Building

Points which are worthy of special consideration when building a model are:

- Take time before you start to thoroughly examine the plan and read the instructions and, if building from a kit, identify the various parts and where they fit. If a particular sequence of assembly is given, follow it unless you have a specific reason for not doing so.
- Pay great attention to any wing joining system, ensuring that it is properly integrated into the rest of the wing structure and not just slotted in as an afterthought.
- Watch the weight. Choose materials carefully – it is easy enough to add ballast but an overweight model will remain an overweight model.
- Keep the tail end and wing tips of the model as light as possible commensurate with

adequate strength; models with light extremities respond better to control inputs.

- Try to contain your natural impatience to see the model finished and work systematically, allowing proper drying time for adhesives.
- Work out the radio installation at an early stage and fit the servos and control surface drives as early as possible during construction.
- Take all possible steps to eliminate slop in control linkages, especially those to elevators and ailerons.
- Have the right tools to hand, in particular: sharp scalpels, a good miniature power drill, plenty of sanding blocks (including a *large* flat one) with various grades of abrasive paper on them and a *flat* building board of adequate size which will accept pins without the use of a hammer!

Pre-flight

Check the longitudinal and lateral balance of the finished model. The longitudinal balance should be as shown on the plan – a little farther forward is usually acceptable, farther back can spell trouble in early flights. The model should balance exactly laterally – add weight to the light tip until it does.

Check that there are no (unintentional) warps in the flying surfaces by viewing them from the front and rear. Any warps must be removed at this stage by gentle application of heat and twisting the surface in opposition to the warp while it cools.

Check that the flying surfaces are correctly aligned with each other and the fuselage in all views. A long straight-edge and a piece of string are essential tools during this phase. At this stage, ensure that the difference in incidence between the wing and tail surfaces is exactly as shown on the plan.

Check that the vertical tail surface (fin and rudder) are properly aligned and not warped.

Check all control surfaces (rudder, elevator, ailerons) to ensure that they are accurately aligned with the fixed surfaces (fin, tailplane, wing) when the controls (both main sticks and trim controls) are in neutral. Adjust as required.

Check operation of all controls for correct sense and the right amount of movement (as specified on the plan). If your transmitter has rate switches on the main functions, set these to give approximately 25 per cent more throw than the normal maximum for use in an emergency.

Check that hatches etc. are properly secured and that batteries and other radio equipment are either fixed or so packed that they cannot shift in flight.

Pick up the model and shake it vigorously. Does anything move? If it does, fix it. Does anything rattle? If it does, find out what and stop it.

Before contemplating flying make sure that the transmitter and receiver batteries are fully charged. Nicads lose charge at a steady rate when not in operation. Do not charge the gear, wait a week or more for the weather and then go out to fly without giving it an extra charge, otherwise the model's first flight, if lengthy, might also be its last!

First flight

If you have not flown an R/C model before, get help from an experienced modeller.

After assembling the model at the field or slope, do a final walk round on it to make sure everything is secure and aligned.

After checking that no-one else is on your frequency, and *only* after this, switch on the transmitter and receiver and check the controls for correct operation and full movement.

For most types of model, a hand glide is worthwhile to check that the trim is approximately right. Exceptions to this are very large or heavy models, where it would be difficult to get the flying speed right from a hand launch giving rise to the risk of a stall from an altitude too low to permit recovery. After all, models do not crash 500 feet up!

Get someone more experienced to do the first launch for you, whether on tow or from a slope. However, do make sure that the person chosen knows how to launch properly. Specifically, when launching from a slope into wind and lift, the model should not be hurled out nose up or it will probably stall.

Concentrate on either keeping the model straight and climbing if on a tow launch (and avoid the temptation to pull in up elevator), or flying straight away from the hill if slope soaring. When the model is off the line, or has gained some height in the slope lift, sort out whether or not you are having to hold in any stick deflections and adjust the trims so that the model is flying properly with the sticks in neutral.

Post flight

After the first flight, do not be content to fly a model which needs offset transmitter trims for straight and level flight: if the control surfaces are at neutral with the trims offset (and they should not be if the pre-flight checking was thoroughly done) adjust them so that the trims can go back to the centre. If surface offset is needed for proper flight find out why. There must be a warp or imbalance somewhere and to correct this with control surface offset is to invite trim problems later when the model is flown at varying speeds and in different conditions.

To get the longest useful life out of your model, keep on top of maintenance tasks. Carry out small repairs immediately on returning from flying – leaving them will often result in a small repair becoming a big one! Keep the model clean, wipe off mud and moisture before putting it in the car for the return journey from the slope or field.

More superficial damage is probably done to models carrying them about than flying them. The effort involved in producing sleeves from bubble-wrap plastic to protect the flying surfaces during transit is well worthwhile. You can go even further by making carrying cases for your models. To make bubble-wrap sleeves, cut the plastic to the required size by folding it over the wing and trimming it off. The open edge of the sleeve, and one end, can then be easily sealed by placing the folded-over sleeve on a flat board and laying a heavy metal straight-edge along the open side, leaving about $3/8$" of plastic protruding. A quick pass along this with an electric paint-stripping heat gun will seal the edges perfectly. Remember to make your sleeves with the bubble on the *inside* for maximum protection.

Nicad batteries have a finite life; every time a battery is charged a fraction of its capacity is lost and eventually it will become impaired to the point where it can no longer hold a useful charge. Treat your batteries properly and you will enjoy several seasons of useful life from them. Do not overcharge them, and when the time comes do not hesitate to replace them – better the small cost of a new nicad than a smashed model and possible accident.

Only when absolutely happy with the model should you start experimenting with small movements of the CG, alterations in wing loading via the addition of ballast and variations of surface incidence setup to get the very best performance out of it. Sometimes quite minor alterations can produce spectacular improvements in performance.

Above all

Do not be afraid to ask more experienced clubmates and modelling friends for help and advice. In my experience this will always be freely given. Remember that what may be a new problem to you will have been confronted and

133

solved many times by other R/C enthusiasts – do not insist on re-inventing the wheel by being too proud to benefit from their efforts. It is my contention that I have made almost every possible mistake connected with the building and flying of model aircraft once – but very few twice!

Enjoy your modelling!

APPENDIX 1

Rule outlines for the major classes

This appendix covers the rule outlines for the major classes of soaring contest flown in the UK. It must be stressed that these are simply summaries of the rules, not the full official ones, which are, in any case, subject to periodic revision. Before either obtaining a model for, or starting to fly in, any particular class, therefore, the full official rules should always be studied. In addition, there are many local variations used by various contest organisers. However, the following should give a basic idea of what is involved in each of the various classes.

General

As a general rule, models must conform to the maximum weights and areas used by the international organising body, the Federation Aeronautique International (FAI), to define what is, or is not, a model aeroplane. From a soaring point of view these can be taken to be a maximum weight of five kilograms and a maximum total flying surface area of approximately 16 square feet. This is not to say that bigger and heavier models than these cannot be flown – in the PSS and scales classes in particular they often are – however, special insurance and "permit to fly" conditions may apply and should be checked first.

Thermal soaring classes

Mini-glider

Model limitations: Maximum wing span 60 inches, maximum weight 22 ounces.
Flying rules: Launch by either hand launch or approved mini-bungee, flight time maximum usually 3 minutes.

Two metre

Model limitations: Maximum span 2 metres (in some club contests for this class, but not all, control functions are limited to rudder and elevator only).
Flying rules: Launch by 150 metre bungee or hand towline. Maximum flight times used vary from five to eight minutes. A landing bonus may or may not be awarded for landing within a 12.5 metre radius circle or on a long "landing tape" laid out into wind.

100S or standard class

Model limitations: Maximum projected span 100 inches.
Flying rules: Launch by 150 metre hand towline or bungee. Flown in "slots" with a duration of eight minutes. Longest flight in the slot receives 1000 points and the rest are scored pro-rata. Landing must be within 150 metres of a designated spot for the flight to count.

BARCS open class

No model limitations.
Flying rules: Launch by 150 metre hand towline only. Flown in "slots" with a duration of ten minutes (fifteen for fly-off rounds). Longest flight in slot scores 1000, rest pro-rata. Minimum of three rounds flown. Top nine (usually) scorers after the rounds fly two further fly-off slots, these scores *only* deciding the top nine places.

Landing within a 12.5 metre radius circle scores 50 bonus points (25 if part of the model is in). Landing outside 75 metres from the centre of the circle scores zero for the flight.

F3J (international) class thermal soaring

No model limitations
Flying rules: Launch by 150 metre hand towline or power winch with 150 metre effective line. Flying rules similar to BARCS open except that multiple re-launches are allowed within the slot (last flight to score) and the landing is on a graduated tape scoring 100 for a landing within 1 metre of the target and reducing to zero outside 20 metres.

F3B (international) class multi-task soaring

No model limitations
Flying rules: Each round consists of three tasks:

Duration – flown to a six minute maximum with a precision landing for bonus points on a graduated tape (as in F3J).

Distance – fly as many laps as possible up and down a 150 metre long course in four minutes.
Speed – fly 2 laps (four legs) of a 150 metre course in the shortest possible time.

The best score in each task receives 1000 points, the rest scoring pro-rata. Launching via a hand towline or electric powered winch. A minimum of three rounds are flown per contest.

Slope soaring

F3F (international) slope speed

No model limitations
Flying rules: Models fly one at a time, against the clock, completing ten legs of a 100 metre long course set out on the ridge. Fastest time in each round receives 1000 points, the rest score pro-rata. A minimum of three rounds are flown per contest.

Sixty inch slope pylon racing

Model limitations: Maximum wing span 60 inches, no other restrictions.
Flying rules: Heats of from two to four models race over ten legs of a 100 metre course, simultaneously. Points are awarded for first, second and third in each heat, semi-finals and a final are held for the top eight scorers after a pre-determined number of rounds.

Slope cross country

No model limitations.
Flying rules: It is impossible to state a definitive set of flying rules for cross-country soaring, as these vary depending upon the nature of the site. Generally, contest organisers set up a series of "gates" on the front and rear sides of the ridge. Contestants must walk around this course while flying their model, performing a pre-defined manoeuvre at each "gate" – a series of turns behind

the gate or a low pass are typical. As the course progresses, the gates are placed farther and farther away from the portion of the site which is producing slope lift, meaning that greater skill is required to complete the required manoeuvre and avoid landing the model due to lack of lift. An overall time limit is set to complete the course, usually between 45 minutes and an hour, course length being typically two to three miles. Points are awarded for each "gate" successfully completed, and usually the top contestants take part in a fly-off around the same, or a re-set different, course.

Some contests permit intermediate landings and re-launches which carry time or point penalties, others do not.

PSS and scale

Model limitations: The model must be a recognisable replica of a full-size power (PSS) or glider aircraft.
Flying rules: These vary widely. Some element of static judging is sometimes (but not always) included; models are usually judged by examining them at a distance of a few yards, known as "stand-off scale" judging. Flight requirements also vary. Many events, especially PSS ones, are run on a "fly-in" basis, with judges or competitors voting for their favourite performers over a whole day's flying. Sailplane scales contests often require a short cross-country flight and a second flight demonstrating the model flying in a scale-like manner.

Slope aerobatics

No model limitations.
Flying rules: These vary from performing a predetermined set of aerobatics in strict sequence to completely free-style performances and "lucky-dip" events in which the competitor draws a card with an aerobatic schedule from a pack "blind" at the beginning of his flight and then attempts to perform this. One or two judges mark each ma-

noeuvre against set criteria and award points, which are sometimes scaled up by a "k" or difficulty factor for each particular figure. Two or three rounds are usually flown, and sometimes a competitor's worst score is dropped.

Electric soaring

F5B (international) class multi-task

Model limitations: Models must comply with a maximum wing loading and maximum battery pack weight, otherwise they are unrestricted.
Flying rules: Each round consists of a single flight, during the first four minutes of which the model must complete as many legs of a 150 metre course as possible, running the electric power unit outside the course only (i.e. all legs are completed while the model is gliding). Points are scored for each leg completed. The model must then make a low pass below a sighting line and then complete a five minute duration flight. Any further use of electric power during this flight is penalised by deducting the seconds of power used from the flight total. A precision landing on a graduated tape for bonus points completes the flight. The total score is given by adding the points scored in the distance, duration and landing elements together, and the round winner scores 1000 points with other competitors scoring pro-rata.

E-slot (electroslot)

Model limitations: Maximum number of cells in battery pack - seven, no other restrictions.
Flying rules: Three rounds are flown, and charging of the flight battery between rounds is not permitted. A number of models fly together in a 12 minute "slot", during which 75 seconds of power run are permitted – any further use of the motor is deducted from the final score, use of the motor beyond 90 seconds in a slot results in a zero score. A precision landing on a graduated

tape terminates the flight for extra points. The slot winner is the pilot returning the highest total of flight plus landing points, and he receives 100 points with the rest scoring pro-rata.

Electroslot E400

Model limitations: Motor must be standard Speed 400 type (380 size motors)
A maximum of seven cells are allowed in the battery pack.
Flying rules: As many rounds as convenient are flown. Charging/changing of flight batteries between rounds is permitted. Scoring is similar to that for E-Slot except that 10 minute slots are used, two minutes of "free" motor run are permitted and there is, usually, no landing requirement.

General

In addition to the above widely recognised classes of competition, most clubs operate their own versions, either in closed club-only contests or in invitation events, and there are an almost limitless number of variations. Always check the rules before you fly!

APPENDIX 2

Sketches showing the major classes

F3F

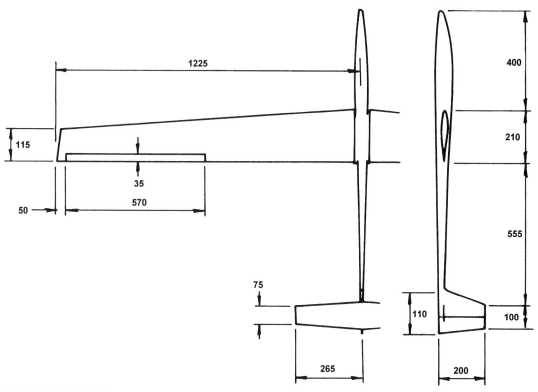

NORWEGIAN STYLE

F3B

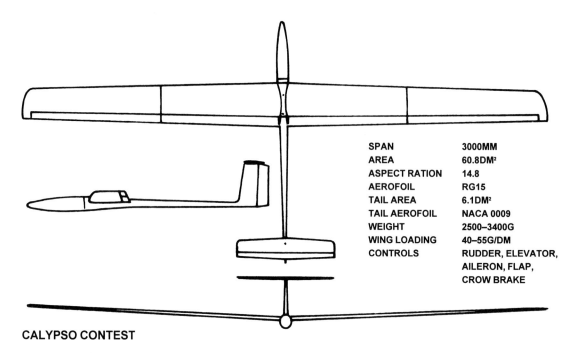

SPAN	3000MM
AREA	60.8DM²
ASPECT RATION	14.8
AEROFOIL	RG15
TAIL AREA	6.1DM²
TAIL AEROFOIL	NACA 0009
WEIGHT	2500–3400G
WING LOADING	40–55G/DM
CONTROLS	RUDDER, ELEVATOR, AILERON, FLAP, CROW BRAKE

CALYPSO CONTEST

F3J opposite page

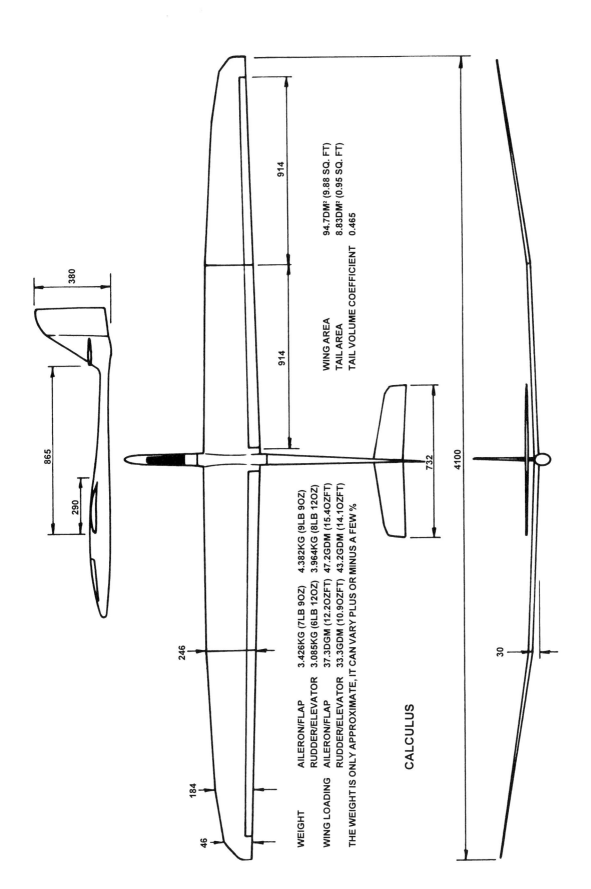

WEIGHT	AILERON/FLAP	3.426KG (7LB 9OZ)	4.382KG (9LB 9OZ)
	RUDDER/ELEVATOR	3.085KG (6LB 12OZ)	3.964KG (8LB 12OZ)
WING LOADING	AILERON/FLAP	37.3DGM (12.2OZFT)	47.2GDM (15.4OZFT)
	RUDDER/ELEVATOR	33.3GDM (10.9OZFT)	43.2GDM (14.1OZFT)

THE WEIGHT IS ONLY APPROXIMATE, IT CAN VARY PLUS OR MINUS A FEW %

WING AREA   94.7DM² (9.88 SQ. FT)
TAIL AREA   8.83DM² (0.95 SQ. FT)
TAIL VOLUME COEFFICIENT 0.465

CALCULUS

G/A R/C glider

SPAN	132IN
O/A LENGTH	76IN
TOTAL LOADING	40Z/SQ. FT
TAIL SPAN	48IN
TOTAL WING AREA	2,300 SQ.IN
AEROFOIL SECTION	NACA 6412

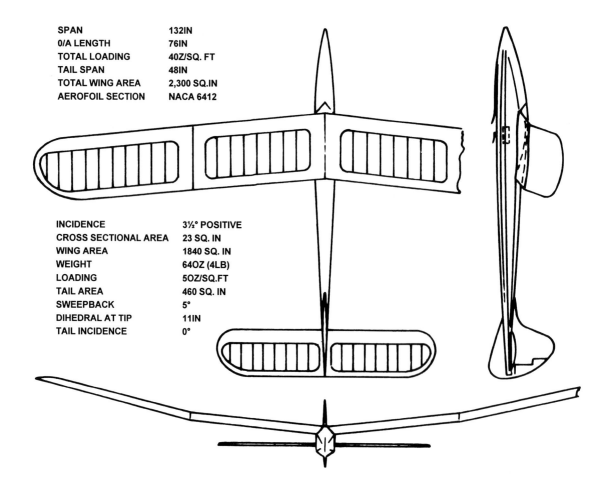

INCIDENCE	3½° POSITIVE
CROSS SECTIONAL AREA	23 SQ. IN
WING AREA	1840 SQ. IN
WEIGHT	64OZ (4LB)
LOADING	5OZ/SQ.FT
TAIL AREA	460 SQ. IN
SWEEPBACK	5°
DIHEDRAL AT TIP	11IN
TAIL INCIDENCE	0°

Slope aerobatic opposite page

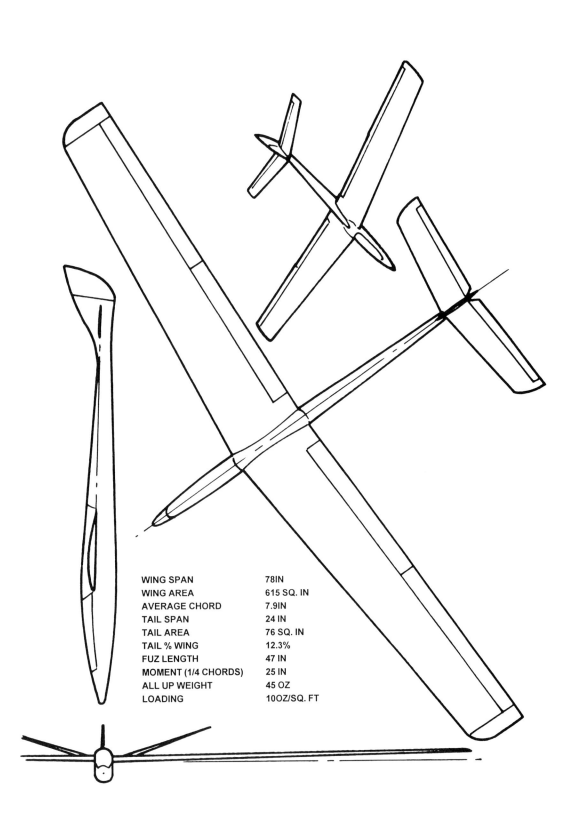

WING SPAN	78IN
WING AREA	615 SQ. IN
AVERAGE CHORD	7.9IN
TAIL SPAN	24 IN
TAIL AREA	76 SQ. IN
TAIL % WING	12.3%
FUZ LENGTH	47 IN
MOMENT (1/4 CHORDS)	25 IN
ALL UP WEIGHT	45 OZ
LOADING	10OZ/SQ. FT

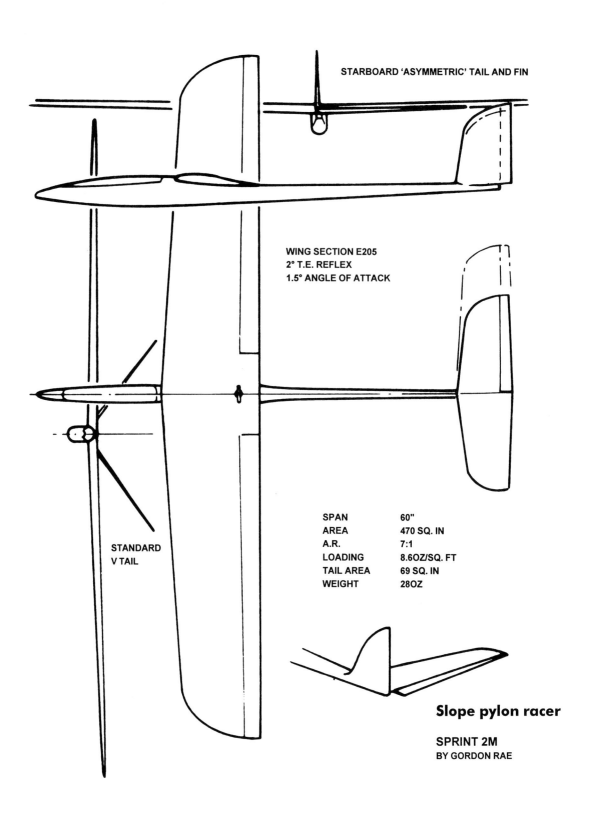

STARBOARD 'ASYMMETRIC' TAIL AND FIN

WING SECTION E205
2° T.E. REFLEX
1.5° ANGLE OF ATTACK

STANDARD
V TAIL

SPAN	60"
AREA	470 SQ. IN
A.R.	7:1
LOADING	8.6OZ/SQ. FT
TAIL AREA	69 SQ. IN
WEIGHT	28OZ

Slope pylon racer

SPRINT 2M
BY GORDON RAE

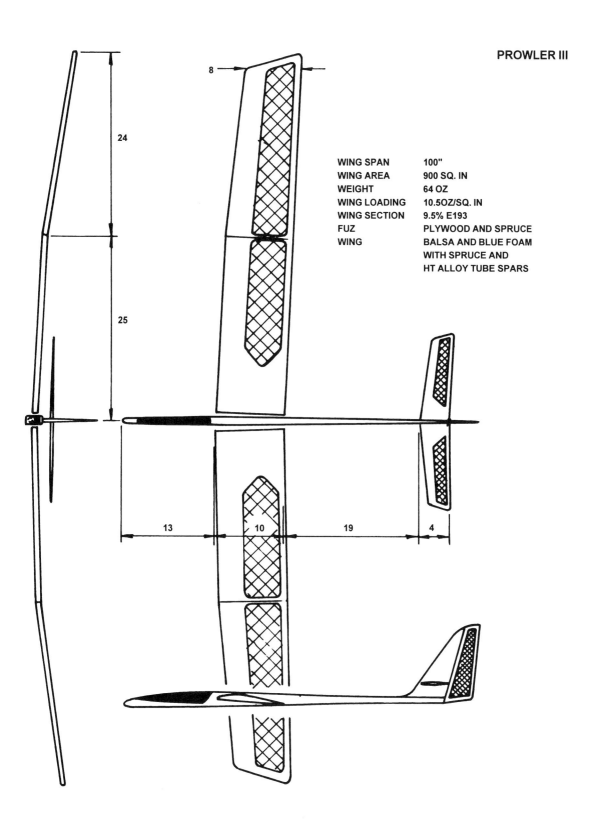

PROWLER III

WING SPAN	100"
WING AREA	900 SQ. IN
WEIGHT	64 OZ
WING LOADING	10.5OZ/SQ. IN
WING SECTION	9.5% E193
FUZ	PLYWOOD AND SPRUCE
WING	BALSA AND BLUE FOAM
	WITH SPRUCE AND
	HT ALLOY TUBE SPARS

8

24

25

13   10   19   4

APPENDIX 3

Names and addresses of organisations

Apart from the local club which every R/C glider pilot will find to be a near essential if he is to derive maximum enjoyment from his flying there are several organisations which he will come across.

The Federation Aeronautique International (FAI)

This international body is responsible for setting up rules for all sporting aviation activities – gliding, parachuting, power flying etc. – throughout the world. The Models Commission of the FAI looks after model matters, in particular establishing rules for new classes and overseeing the organisation, by specific member countries, of European and World Championships in the International classes. It is inappropriate to give an address for the FAI because members are the national bodies (BMFA in the case of the UK) and individuals have no reason to have direct contact with the FAI.

The British Model Flying Association (BMFA)

The body recognised by the Royal Aeroclub as representing model flying in the UK. Many clubs are affiliated to the BMFA, and through them their members are automatically covered by approved third party insurance. Membership of the BMFA is worthwhile for everyone who has an interest in model flying, as only by presenting a strong and united front are meaningful negotiations with national bodies (such as the Civil Aviation Authority) possible when matters concerning the regulation and control of model flying are raised. Through the auspices of the BMFA the National Championships in all model flying classes are run each year.

BMFA
General Secretary
Chacksfield House
31 St. Andrews Road
Leicester LE2 8RE

The British Association of Radio Controlled Soarers (BARCS)

Unlike the BMFA, this national body represents individual members rather than affiliated clubs. Over the last twenty-five years it has been influential in setting the pattern for competitive R/C soaring, and it was largely through BARCS efforts, in concert with the BMFA, that the F3J class of international thermal soaring came into being.

BARCS
Membership Secretary
36 Windmill Avenue
Wokingham
Berks RG41 3XD
email: brian@skyquest.demon.co.uk

The British Electric Flight Association (BEFA)
This body performs a similar function to BARCS for electric flight enthusiasts.
BEFA
Membership Secretary
123 Lane End Road
High Wycombe
Bucks HP12 4HF

The Society of Antique Modellers, Chapter 35 (SAM35)
A group of vintage enthusiasts, many of whom are interested in free-flight modelling, but who also have a healthy radio control interest. They publish an excellent monthly newsletter.
SAM35
Membership Secretary
Vine House
22 Hollins Lane
Marple Bridge
Stockport
Cheshire SK6 5BJ

APPENDIX 4

Balsa wood weight and density

Sheet size	Imperial thickness (in.)	Metric thickness (mm)	Weight (g)						
			Ultra light 65kg/m³ (4lb/ft³)	Very light 95kg/m³ (6lb/ft³)	Light 127kg/m³ (8lb/ft³)	Medium 160kg/m³ (10lb/ft³)	Med./Hard 192kg/m³ (12lb/ft³)	Hard 225kg/m³ (14lb/ft³)	Very hard 320kg/m³ (20lb/ft³)
3" × 36"	1/32	0.8	4	5	7	9	11	12	18
	1/16	1.5	7	11	14	18	21	25	35
	3/32	2.4	11	16	21	27	32	37	53
	1/8	3.0	14	21	28	35	43	50	71
	3/16	4.8	21	32	43	53	64	74	106
	1/4	6.4	28	43	57	71	85	99	142
	5/16	7.9	35	53	71	89	106	124	177
	3/8	9.5	43	64	85	106	128	149	213
	1/2	12.7	57	85	114	142	170	199	284
4" × 36" and 3" × 48"	1/32	0.8	5	7	9	12	14	17	24
	1/16	1.6	9	14	19	24	28	33	47
	3/32	2.4	14	21	28	35	43	50	71
	1/8	3.2	19	28	38	47	57	66	95
	3/16	4.8	28	43	57	71	85	99	142
	1/4	6.4	38	57	76	95	114	132	189
	5/16	7.9	47	71	95	118	142	166	236
	3/8	9.5	57	85	114	142	170	199	284
	1/2	12.7	76	114	151	189	227	265	378
4" × 48"	1/32	0.8	6	9	13	16	19	22	32
	1/16	1.6	13	19	25	32	38	44	63
	3/32	2.4	19	28	38	47	57	66	95
	1/8	3.2	25	38	50	63	76	88	126
	3/16	4.8	38	57	76	95	114	132	189
	1/4	6.4	50	76	101	126	151	177	252
	5/16	7.9	63	95	126	158	189	221	315
	3/8	9.5	76	114	151	189	227	265	378
	1/2	12.7	101	151	202	252	303	353	504

BRITAIN'S MOST POPULAR MODEL AIRCRAFT MAGAZINES

Over 1.3 million readers a year can't be wrong!

Have you seen how good they are lately?